But Who Are We Now?

Strategies and Stories for Boomers and Beyond

Susan Dean, PhD

Cover and interior design by Kurt A. Dierking II

Published by Authors Unite Publishing

ISBN: 978-1-960346-75-9

But Who Are We Now?

Strategies and Stories for Boomers and Beyond

Susan Dean, PhD

AUTHORSUNITE

For Skylar, Morgan, and Hannah, with love

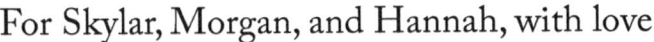

"Give the ones you love wings to fly, roots to come back and
reasons to stay"

—Dalai Lama

"We delight in the beauty of the butterfly, but rarely admit the changes it has gone through to achieve that beauty"

—Maya Angelou

Author's Note

The birth of the Baby Boom Generation—more than 77.5 million Americans—spanned 1946 to 1964. The early boomers, those born between 1946 and 1954, were impacted more by the conservatism of the fifties, while the younger boomers were directly influenced by their leading-edge predecessors. The first-stage boomers are in their early to late seventies now, while the youngest are in their sixties.

When I began writing this book, we were just trying to acclimatize to a global pandemic. COVID-19 had clearly changed the game. The virus called upon us to be creative and think alternatively, steering our lives going forward. My greatest hope is that by the time you are reading this, our lives will have become freer of COVID and its variant viruses and that we will, therefore, find ourselves a bit less challenged, or at least less restricted.

Contents

Introduction

"I never think of the future—it comes soon enough"
— Albert Einstein

We are the Baby Boom Generation, the ruling aristocracy of our people, who thought we had it all, knew it all, and would always reign. We had a kind of arrogance that fuels change and greatness. But we perhaps did not foresee a possible abdication of the throne.

Through our lens, love would rule. But the war raged on, both on foreign shores and in our households, between us and our government, between us and our parents, and sometimes between us and ourselves. Our youth was a time of great revolution. We bucked authority and establishment, rewrote the rules for socializing and proselytizing, and wore our convictions like a badge of honor. The floodgates had opened—and we were not walking gently through but were crashing forth with inexorable speed.

On foreign shores, battles were waged. But here at home, we were fighting for love—free, alternative, and without guile. We sported love beads, staged love-ins, and sang to the loss of innocence. We were the flower children, whose blossoms seemed eternal. We gave and made love openly, without expectation, without regret. We communed with love, gave birth to love children, and insisted that love was the answer.

But what was the question? And exactly where and when were we derailed?

We navigated our lives with unbridled enthusiasm as King shared his dream, Twiggy donned a miniskirt, and Elvis's hips were upstaged by Mick's. We luxuriated in a spiritual bath of Eastern philosophy, hypnosis, psychoanalysis, astrology, and hallucinogens. We, who feasted on an optimism born of a thriving world economy, were poised to speak out for peace and equality. We could not be coerced into a world that had come before us. We would make our own new universe. We took a stand. During the counterculture of the sixties and seventies, women and persons of color were fighting for equal rights, educating themselves on political issues, and revising the handbook on how to live and what to say. We were, after all, about to change history in a very big way. And the world as we knew it would bear little resemblance to itself going forward.

Or so we believed.

Who of us jumped on the wagon train of tuning in, turning on, and dropping out? The counterculture that the cultural norms of the fifties spawned gave us an enormous opening to investigate our curiosities and fantasies. When men like Ginsburg and Leary touted LSD and free love meant "have at it" sex, decisions were to be made. Boomers were commanded to be hip and, thus, hippies. Nudity was de rigueur at music festivals and other social gatherings, and those who stayed clothed often felt self-conscious and out of step.

Peer pressure can never be underestimated. Not all boomers signed on to become hippies. Make no mistake, however. The movement was on, and there was no indication that the social attitudes would return to the conservatism of the fifties. Women were seductive in topless bathing suits and see-through blouses sans bras. Individuals were experimenting with multiple sex partners, engaging in open marriages, and attending clubs that held orgies. Pornographic films came out of the shadows, and Broadway shows featured actors who were totally nude. I know. I attended opening night of *Hair*. These new freedoms were, for many of us, confusing and scary, and we saw our personal values under self-scrutiny. As much as we thought ourselves to be doing our own thing, the truth is that we were following the rhythm of the times—to be free, spread love, and wear a flower in our hair.

But who are we now, and how do we translate our individual blueprint? Are we still fighting for the same causes and values? Do we still want love and peace? How have our distinctive victories and losses brought us to this moment? We know now that we are not invincible, just like those before us, despite our rich pedigree. It is understood that we can enjoy the memories. But we cannot bask in them, for today is our challenge. We have tired of all the clichés about how fast time flies and how we must live every day as if it is our last. We are painfully aware of these sentiments.

How do we feel relevant at a time when, all too often, it seems as though someone hit the Delete key on us? We had ambitions and dreams and hopes for what our lives would become after traversing the ambiguous slopes of our youth. But how frequently do we find ourselves thinking that our lives did not turn out the way we had imagined back when everything was *groovy*? Life might have exceeded our expectations or, conversely, left us feeling grossly disappointed. Either way, here we are, still trying to defy the odds.

Sixty is the new forty! Really? Who started that marketing campaign? Sixty is sixty...make no mistake, with all the weight and all the bonuses. And who penned the term *a woman of a certain age*? Why can't we just say our age without fear of judgment, embarrassment, or gossip? Or how about the television commercial for seniors advertising a protein drink with the tagline "Age is just a number, and mine is unlisted." This is indicative of the pressure older women still feel to conceal themselves and their age.

However, rather than shy away from our age and hide the years we have lived, we must wear them proudly. Legend has it that we have all the complexities and all the robustness of a full-bodied cabernet sauvignon and all the crispness and vibrance of a sauvignon blanc. We just need to uncork that bottle, embrace where we are now, and run with it—or walk slowly and carefully.

There is no question that there was a large price to pay for many of us who *really lived* the sixties and seventies. Some straddled the line, others crossed it like racehorses. And when we were in it, we were voraciously committed. However, at some point, the music died for a second time, and we had to figure out our next act. For many, this has been daunting. We baby boomers had a specific idea of how our lives would be. We were activists, and when we protested, we believed our lives would be going in a new direction.

But things didn't always go as planned. Some of us have had good lives while others have struggled. However, I contend that there is always hope, whether it relies on an attitude shift or a commitment to do the hard work.

In the following pages, I will discuss some of the losses we have experienced and share ideas on living and how you can maximize your life as a boomer. Finally, we will probe that elusive commodity—love.

I

LOSS

A Garden Beyond Paradise

Everything you see has its roots in the unseen world.
The forms may change,
yet the essence remains the same.
Every wondrous sight will vanish,
every sweet word will fade.
But do not be disheartened,
The Source they come from is eternal—
growing, branching out,
giving new life and new joy.
Why do you weep?—
That Source is within you,
and this whole world is springing up from it.
The Source is full,
its waters are ever-flowing;
Do not grieve,
drink your fill!
Don't think it will ever run dry—
This is the endless Ocean!

— Rumi

When Loss Comes Calling

Throughout our lifetimes, we will experience countless losses, many of them unidentified as such. They often hide inside depression, addiction, and isolation rather than jumping out and identifying themselves as we take roll call. Feelings of inadequacy and low self-worth are frequent outgrowths. But what do we know about the true essence of loss? And if we cannot clarify our losses, how do we grieve them?

It is also possible that we are not emotionally equipped to deal with our grief. Many of us have no idea how to process feelings of loss, and too often, the consequences are severe. All of the platitudes about moving on or how time will heal are just empty, ineffective phrases and come across as gratuitous and not helpful to the griever. How do we even recognize each loss, not to mention process all the feelings that accompany it? When we lose a family member, partner, friend, pet, or any loved one, we mourn the relationship that has ended. Whether we are terminated from a job, are forced to forfeit our home, experience health challenges, or see our lifestyle compromised, there is a great sense of loss, grief, and failure.

In my work as a grief and loss specialist, I have been struck by an overarching theme of grief and loss among boomers. Despite all the otherwise great aspects of the boomer years, substantial heart-wrenching loss has accompanied them. The significance of this subject warrants a full section of its own, as you will see. I am going to touch on some of the grief areas just to give you a window into the hearts and minds of those who belong to this very special generation.

It is important to take an honest look at some of the many losses we experience and how we are or are not grieving them. It is not necessary to spend a lot of time on each. But it's essential to examine them just a bit. Keep in mind that each story has a timeline of its own. Some people suffer for a few months while others struggle with their loss over a period of years. Each griever experiences loss in a highly individual way. As a coach, I can listen to, empathize with, and support my clients. As a writer, I will depict their stories in an anecdotal fashion. The only story I can tell in graphic detail is my own.

As my process with grievers is not therapy, my clients' participation is very much what drives their recovery. *Recovery* sounds a bit like recuperation from an illness, and while grief is hardly an illness, it can be paralyzing and debilitating and contribute to physical illness and emotional distress. Though grief is not a malady, there too often are disproportionate feelings of shame, guilt, remorse, panic, and hopelessness assigned to it. According to *Psychiatric Times*, by age sixty-five, more than half of American women and 10 percent of American men will have been widowed at least once. One month after a major loss, about 40 percent of the bereaved meet the criteria for a major depressive episode. Two months after the loss, 24 percent meet these criteria. Newly bereaved individuals have a nine times higher risk of major depression than their married counterparts.[1]

With the clear link between loss and major depression, it is apparent that boomers are particularly vulnerable to diminishing mental health as we are hit with all different kinds of loss from what, at times, feels like every angle.

I cannot emphasize enough that if you are laboring with grief that lasts and disrupts your ability to engage, it is vital to seek help from a clinician who specializes in grief, loss, and trauma work.

1 Paula J. Clayton, MD, and Paula L. Hensley, MD, "Bereavement-Related Depression," *Psychiatric Times* 25 no. 8 (2008): https://www.psychiatrictimes.com/view/bereavement-related-depression.

In Plain Sight

It is difficult to quantify losses, especially when you try to compare which ones are worse than others. All loss is sad and troubling, and grief is an emotion we would rather avert. But for boomers, I think one loss that cannot be overstated is loss of relevance.

We were on top of our game for so long that nothing could touch us. Everything we did seemed to matter, whether it was marching for civil rights or stringing beads. It was a time when world events were truly substantive. Sit-ins and love-ins were commonplace. The Evangelical movement gained traction as a response to our audacity. Authority was questioned in just about every arena. Indifference just wasn't an option. And it was the children of the fifties and early sixties who would get seduced into the maelstrom of change. We invented it! Or so we thought.

Technology was becoming more advanced when we sent a man to the moon. Black people daringly sat down at lunch counters and entered schools specifically designated for white people. Newness was infiltrating our psyches. And somehow, we were the purveyors of it all. We were that smug. We struggled over US involvement in the Vietnam War, but we were free from the attachment to World War II. We were an involved, contemplative, engaged cohort who truly cared about every facet of life. And we took a stand.

Now, fast-forward to the present. How relevant do you feel when twenty-one-year-olds are making six figures straight out of college because they created an app? Or when a teenager is making a small fortune while trending on social media? We ache for substance, for a country with values and fairness, and for the days when everything we did seemed important. We now long to see more meaning in the world. Our hearts ache for civility.

Were we kidding ourselves with our self-importance?

My contention is no. The changes we forged were epic. And as boomers, we saw much of that change take effect. When we saw the federal legalization of gay marriage in 2014, we thought back to the gay liberation movement we passionately spearheaded in the 1960s. As we witness more women speaking up and having a voice through movements such as #MeToo, we are reminded of Gloria Steinem, the women's rights movement, and how we fought for Roe and gathered by the thousands to protest anti-abortion laws in Central Park.[2]

We watch the seeds we planted sprouting in so many progressive movements today: gay rights, women's rights, environmental causes, advancement of space travel, and the increased use of electricity and solar power out of respect for the environment. We are the generation that gave momentum to great change, which was prescient in our cries. But the battles we once valiantly fought are not yet won.

As the champions of the civil rights movement, we are failing miserably with the state of things right now. Before we passed the torch to the next generation, the Civil Rights Act was put into effect in 1964, outlawing discrimination based on race, color, religion, gender, national origin, and, eventually, sexual orientation and gender identity.

We moved that dial only to see it become antithetical to what we strived for and still have not yet achieved. It was easy to believe that our generation would be the one to usher in the greatest revamping of society. Yet as the years have passed, we are confronted with the fact that, in many ways, our work is far from done. For every injustice we fought to correct, we learned of more ways the world is increasingly prejudiced and without equity.

---

2 Daniel K. Williams, "What You Don't Know About the Abortion Fight in America Before *Roe v. Wade*," *Time*, January 4, 2016, https://time.com/4154084/anti-abortion-pre-roe/.

Turn up the Volume

S o, what can we, as boomers, do to still be pertinent and participate in the important movements and discussions going on today? We are never too old to make meaningful changes. We can join UNESCO, add another voice in the fight against racial injustice, and be a force for its cause. UNESCO uses education, science, and culture to inform, inspire, and engage people everywhere to foster understanding and respect for each other and our planet. In 1978, the *Declaration on Race and Racial Prejudice* reaffirmed that "All human beings belong to a single species and are descended from a common stock. They are born equal in dignity and rights and all an integral part of humanity."[3]

If you marched for equality, voted with your conscience, or fought for the rights of all humans in your youth, it's important to remember that the fight isn't over. Nor is it yet lost. There is much you can do today to support the work you and your fellow boomers began in the sixties. Consider learning more about and contributing to the following efforts to right wrongs in our country and our world.

- In 2021, the United Nations Human Rights Council adopted a milestone UN resolution to create an independent mechanism, made up of three experts, to investigate the

3 UNESCO, Declaration on race and racial prejudice, 1978.

root causes of systemic racism and police violence. A year later, The UN Committee on the Elimination of Racial Discrimination expressed concern over the brutality and use of excessive or deadly force by law enforcement. It asked our country specifically to create or strengthen independent oversight bodies to ensure accountability of law enforcement officials for inappropriate use of force.[4]

- What about the Supreme Court ruling to overturn *Roe v. Wade*? Did any of us ever imagine that could even happen? At this moment, it is incumbent upon each state to establish laws protecting abortion rights, as there is no federal standard. Some states make it illegal to have an abortion or consider criminal penalties if a woman tries to obtain one. In those states, pregnant women who do not want to go full-term will face the dilemma of doing jail time or traveling to a state that allows abortions. Of course, women of lesser means often do not have the finances to support that travel.

- *Our Bodies, Ourselves* was published in 1973 as a groundbreaking book that stressed the importance of women claiming their own bodies and gave each of us permission to choose how we would honor what was undeniably ours. In concert with the feminist movement, women were encouraged to take charge of their physicality and feel comfortable in their own skin. Now we have lived to see that personal dignity once again on the chopping block. In July 2023, however, the Federal Drug Administration approved a nonprescription birth control pill for use in the US. That is a big win for future unplanned pregnancies.

---

4 The website for the United Nations Human Rights Office of the High Commissioner.

The Mirror Doesn't Lie

And then, here comes ageism. There is no doubt that ageism is alive and well, but we must prevail and prove to the younger generations that they cannot obliterate us easily, though many have tried. It is imperative that we speak out against ageism at every turn, especially in the workplace. The Federal Equal Employment Opportunity Commission (EEOC) said in a 2018 report that age-based harassment claims more than tripled between 1992 and 2017.[5] A national survey of 3,900 workers by AARP Research in 2018 found that nearly one person in four had heard a boss or a colleague make a negative age-based remark about them.[6] How rude!

Journal of the American Geriatrics Society has become more sensitive to age-related biases. In an editorial post in June 2017, the editors stated, "Despite years of progress in our own understanding of aging, public perceptions are still mired in a swamp that treats aging as undesirable. The public associates aging almost exclusively with decline and deterioration."[7]

5 Victoria A. Lipnic, *The State of Age Discrimination and Older Workers in the U.S. 50 Years After the Age Discrimination in Employment Act (ADEA)* (U.S. Equal Employment Opportunity Commission, 2018).

6 Perron, Rebecca, *The Value of Experience: Age Discrimination Against Older Workers Persists* (AARP, 2018), https://www.aarp.org/content/dam/aarp/research/surveys_statistics/econ/2018/value-of-experience-age-discrimination-highlights.doi.10.26419-2Fres.00177.002.pdf.

7 Nancy E. Lundebjerg, MPA, Daniel E. Trucil, MA, MPH, Emily C. Hammond, BA, and William B. Applegate, MD, MPH, "When It Comes to Older Adults, Language Matters: *Journal of the American Geriatrics Society* Adopts Modified American Medical Association Style," *Journal of the American Geriatric Society* 65 no. 7 (2017): 1386-88.

However, in a 2024 poll conducted by the Pew Research Center, the fastest-growing age group in the US workforce consists of people seventy-five and older.[8] Data shows that more Americans are working well past retirement age for several reasons, including high costs and low savings. Forecasters expect the cohort of workers past age seventy-five to double over the next decade as retirement plans evolve away from pensions that encouraged workers to retire by sixty-five.[9]

Some older individuals might struggle to relate to certain movements and process progressive ideas, particularly because they are so often led by the youngest generations. For that reason, activism might appear to be a young person's game, so we are often reluctant to get involved. However, as boomers, it is imperative that we have agency in the important dialogues that need to happen. Those of us who have graduated to being seniors have the credibility and years to have these meaningful conversations with our peers. Perhaps discussing modern-day movements with our friends and family, including the younger ones, might make today's progressive ideas feel more accessible and less intimidating to those who believe their days of advocacy are behind them.

Despite being pioneers, we definitely lack street cred today. We are unequivocally considered the *old folks* who are being replaced by millennials, Gen Xers, and Gen Y, and it erodes our egos. A new generation has surpassed us in numbers, and we need to graciously welcome them all and try to understand them. They blasted through with technology that was bewildering, challenging, and terrifying but also life-changing in many positive ways. We were given new vehicles to communicate face-to-face with friends and family. With the growing diaspora of children moving away from family, it is a blessing to be able to get on a Zoom call and see our children and

8 Katherine Schaeffer, "U.S. centenarian population is projected to quadruple over the next 30 years," January 29, 2024, Pew Research Center website, https://www.pewresearch.org/short-reads/2024/01/09/us-centenarian-population-is-projected-to-quadruple-over-the-next-30-years/.

9 Angela M. Antonelli, "The Aging of America: A Changing Picture of Work and Retirement," March 2018, Georgetown University McCourt School of Public Policy website, https://cri.georgetown.edu/the-aging-of-america-a-changing-picture-of-work-and-retirement/#:~:text=Older%20Americans%20Are%20Working%20Longer,to%20work%20past%20age%2065.

grandchildren. Of course, with invention comes resistance to the learning curve of something new, although we must—even though we cannot compete with two-year-olds on iPads. But here's the thing: It is not about competition. We must embrace forward thinking and new technology if we are to stay in the game. Plain and simple. No time for lamentation.

For many of us, it has not been easy to see our children cohabitate with their love interests before marriage, especially those with children. But it is their way. We do not necessarily believe in their parenting styles, though they seem self-assured. Please know that none of this is judgment. It's merely observation. I have a feeling many of you are nodding in agreement. We can only hope that our children and grandchildren will have good values, avoid many of the bad choices we made, and make all the good ones.

But such is the way of life. Each generation kind of morphs into the next—some more gracefully and willingly than others.

Relationship Is Not Guaranteed

W e felt free. Free to be you. Free to be me. Free to love who we wanted, when we wanted. And with that freedom came a price. Many families were splintered. It was easy to break the wedding vows—perhaps too easy. Often, couples with children lived separately. Some kept their nice homes, while others scaled down considerably. Couples who were friends with the divorced couple frequently chose sides after the divorce. Many asked, "Which partner do we remain friends with, and how will we let the other partner know that the friendship is over?" Sad, but commonly, this was the case. Divorce typically brings with it some form of stigma or feelings of failure.

Roughly one in three boomers are unmarried.[10] Widowhood and never marrying are factors. But declining boomer marriage rates are mostly because of divorce. Divorce has been a game changer for boomers and their future. Between 1990 and 2012, the divorce rate for those between fifty-five and sixty-four more than doubled, while the rate of divorce among people over the age of sixty-five nearly tri-

---

10 Susan L. Brown and I-Fen Lin, "Unmarried Boomers Confront Old Age: A National Portrait," *The Gerontologist* 52, no. 2 (2012).

pled. Even as the baby boomers continue to age, they divorce more than any other age group. "The gray divorce" refers to the divorce of couples generally aged fifty and above who had been married for a significant amount of time. [11]

There are many reasons and possible explanations posited for the increase in divorce among older adults. The surge in gray divorce is one possibly unintended consequence of longevity. The lengthening of life expectancies decreases the likelihood that marriages will end in death, creating a broader window of time for couples to be exposed to the risk of divorce.[12] My position has always been that the vow "Till death do we part" was created when a lifespan was likely thirty-five or forty years—approximately half of what it is now. It was more realistic then that couples could fulfill that vow.

The weakening norm of marriage as a lifelong institution, combined with an emphasis on individualism and personal fulfillment, might have contributed to the increase in divorce among older adults. As we age and enter various stages of life, some couples might simply cease to meet one another's needs the way they once did. As boomers, we grew up in a time when the institution of marriage appeared infallible—an indestructible pillar of society. However, we have since seen firsthand how this belief might have been a bit naive or misguided.

Kevin

Kevin was a devoted father of two sons. He always looked forward to taking them to their sports activities, talking about their school day, and tucking them in at night. He and his wife of fifteen years lived in a small, close-knit community. She was a good mom, always had a hot meal for the family at dinnertime, and devoted much of her time to community activities.

---

11 Susan L. Brown and I-Fen Lin, "The Gray Divorce Revolution: Rising Divorce Among Middle-Aged and Older Adults," *The Journals of Gerontology* 67, no. 6 (2012).
12 Ibid.

Kevin thought they were a very happy couple until his wife came home one day and announced that she wanted a divorce. She had fallen in love with someone else. And not only that—she wanted a place of her own without custody of the children. Kevin was blindsided. He could not imagine what this would look like and how he would bring up the boys on his own.

His life was completely upended, which meant he had to start thinking very quickly about logistics for operations going forward—getting the children to and from school, extracurricular activities, lunchboxes and dinnertime, homework and bedtime—all while holding down his full-time job. "I felt shame and disgrace," he said, "not just for myself but for my boys as well. Soon, everyone would learn about my wife's affair because, in a small town, it was impossible to keep gossip at bay."

It would take time and effort to reconstruct his new role in the family. Kevin had to make many adjustments to keep the family intact and perform his work in concert with his parenting duties. His feelings of loss weighed heavily on him as he tried to grasp the enormity of his new normal.

Unexpectedly, as the months passed, a calm washed over him, and he grew to embrace his new routine of running an all-male household. "I actually started to feel happier once I gradually let go of my sorrow and heartache over my breakup," he said.

Kevin's story is one of countless in our generation. As a wave of individualism breathes into society, we can expect that many of the partners we thought would be with us for life leave us for their own paths. By becoming aware of this reality—that perhaps marriage may not be as solid an institution as we once thought—we can embrace our originality and see ourselves as important and worthy, separate from our partnerships.

Tanya

Tanya solicited my help after a very messy divorce. You know the deal: husband and younger female colleague, late nights at the office... blah, blah, blah. We have heard it ad nauseam. Yet the sting is raw and red hot when it happens to you.

Tanya wondered how she would move on. Her life had been inextricably defined by her marriage. Wed in the sixties, she and her husband grew up together, went to rallies and marches together, mourned JFK, RFK, and MLK together, had babies, went to graduations and weddings—*always* together. She was scared and lost, and she did not know how to negotiate the two. So many memories of a life so full had been stolen from her in plain sight. Her anger and fear were preventing her from grieving. Focusing on how she would malign her ex and retaliate in any and every way possible was using up all her energy and keeping her from looking at herself.

And yet, she was not quite clear about her loss. In our work together, her lack of clarity became increasingly apparent. It was not as obvious as she initially believed. Yes, her marriage had ended. But in that, so had her personal identity. The perky, cheeky, sixties feminist hat she'd always worn was now drooping and faded. She was one-half of a package. She was 50 percent of a couple. Her scrapbook was filled with *we* and *us* memories, but now she was reduced to *I* and *me*.

She confided that maybe her marriage, which had bordered on banal, had been at least something she could count on and had planned on having for the rest of her life. She loved her husband, for better or for worse. He was familiar. At this juncture, she was forced to consider who she was as a stand-alone person, and that was terrifying. While in her relationship, she'd never noticed that she had let her sense of self slip away. It was clear that she needed to grieve that loss and find her way back.

Oliver

An inconsolable sixty-four-year-old man sought my help to discuss the loss of his best friend. They had hiked together, swam in the ocean, took trips to the mountains, skied, golfed, and played on the same teams since grade school. His friend went to sleep one evening and never woke up. Oliver was shattered. He felt less than whole without him. I recommended that he take it slow. He cried, and I cried with him. I held him close and told him to not be afraid. Oliver had been carrying this loss around with him for two years.

This was not a lost wallet or cell phone that can easily be replaced. His friend was a living, giving, loving part of his life, and he needed time to grieve the loss and feel complete with that relationship. There is no such thing as replacing one relationship with another. When people do that on the rebound, it is illogical and a recipe for failure. You simply cannot replace a living being with another living being. It takes time to grieve, and we must go through the grieving process before we move forward.

We met each week, as he just wanted a space in which to talk about his friend and the time they'd shared. That was important to him, and in truth, it is an important part of being able to discharge the grief. We looked at photos of the many aspects that documented their journey, from Boy Scouts to wine tastings and so much along the way. I studied his expressions as he recalled the years, which went from the saddest to the magnificent.

In time, Oliver worked toward saying goodbye to his pal—not ever forgetting him or the times they shared—so he could go on with his life. I am happy to report that he called me some months after our work together concluded to tell me that he was starting to be more social and form friendships with other men. He still thought of his special friend from time to time. But now when he did, it was a reflection on all the fun times they'd shared, filled with gratitude that he'd had his friendship.

Still Rising

Admittedly, an overwhelming consequence of *free love* was the great number of marriages that dissolved. Couples were tossing their keys in the middle of a circle and playing what looked like children's games, but with each other's spouses and without guile. Women were becoming equal opportunists in the bedroom, and the pill helped level the playing field. Whatever he could do, so could she without the risk of pregnancy.

While these concerns might seem out of step by today's standards, the women's movement gave rise to a freedom that was often muddled and misused. The race was on! It was women vs. men. To some, this truly was the battle. But far too many women who entered the race did not address the inherent consequences, unforeseen and challenging at best. The competition for equal status pushed many women so vigorously toward a finish line that they landed in a ditch. Divorce had almost become *fashionable*, easy to attain, and seemingly preferable to staying in unfulfilling marriages.

Boomers mostly married in the sixties and seventies and divorced in the eighties and nineties and beyond. Divorce was so rampant that I assert that many of the offspring of divorce married later in life than their parents because they'd lived as children of shattered families. In the 1960s, the median age of first marriage for both men and women was in the early twenties. [13] Between 2014 and 2018, the median age of first marriage for men and women was 29.7 and 27.9, respectively.[14] According to the U.S. Census Bureau, as of 2024, it rose to 30.2 years for men and 28.6 for women.[15] The age at which couples first dive into marriage is on the rise, perhaps a product of our increasingly individualistic lifestyle or exposure to the increasing divorce rates in the boomer generation.

Furthermore, a rising female labor force in the past few decades has given women more economic autonomy, allowing them to support themselves outside marriage. However, splitting up on the brink of retirement can still be financially catastrophic. Although our parents and their parents before them might have been in unhappy marriages, it was less common for women to get up and go! They did not have too many options beyond being wives and mothers. But the climate was changing. When women were asked at cocktail parties what they did for a living, it had become embarrassing to respond, "Oh, I'm just a housewife and mother." Just a mother, indeed! Without question, motherhood is the most important job of all, but women felt *less than* if they were not active players in the professional or business world.

I bless all the women who were the mavericks of the women's movement. My life felt indelibly changed for the better because of Gloria Steinem and Ms. magazine. And what about *The Feminine Mystique*? Betty Friedan's activism and feminism opened our minds to endless possibilities. And we cannot forget pioneer Simone de Beauvoir, who gave us *The Second Sex*. Although it took years for her to jump on the feminist bandwagon, she ultimately concluded that the goal of feminism was to transform society and women's place in it. Doors long closed to us were starting to unlatch, and we walked through, some of us courageously and some of us with consternation.

The Equal Pay Act of 1963 was passed to protect women from gender wage inequality between themselves and their male

---

13 D'Vera Cohn, "Marriage Rate Declines and Marriage Age Rises," December 14, 2011, Pew Research Center website, https://www.pewresearch.org/social-trends/2011/12/14/marriage-rate-declines-and-marriage-age-rises/.

14 Population Reference Bureau. "Median Age at First Marriage (Women)." Dataset 2015-1019. https://www.prb.org/usdata/indicator/marriage-age-women/snapshot/.

15 United States Census Bureau, "Nearly Two-Thirds of U.S. Households Are Family Households," news release, November 12, 2024.

counterparts who were doing the same exact job. According to data agglomerated by the Economic Policy Institute, the average woman earned 62.4 cents on average to the male dollar in 1979. Even though the wage gap between men and women has narrowed in the past few decades, it most certainly still exists. As of 2016, a typical working woman was paid 83 cents compared to the dollar earned by her male coworkers. The average woman loses more than $530,000 throughout her lifetime due to the gender wage gap. That number is $800,000 for college-educated working women. This gap likely plays a large role in the retirement insecurity faced particularly by older women.[16]

Linda

Linda was used to the good life. She and her husband were members of a country club, where much of their social life was centered. They dined there four or five times a week. Linda played tennis while her husband golfed. Together, they shared in a weekly bridge game. Their gorgeous home was in his name, as he'd owned it before they married. Suddenly, he wanted her to leave. Another woman had grabbed his attention, and he chose to live with her. He felt his wife had enjoyed the benefit of a free ride for way too long, and they had a prenup in his favor. When they divorced, she no longer had access to the club. She was cut off abruptly from the lifestyle she had become accustomed to, and she felt rejected, shattered, and depressed.

It was enough to deal with divorce and all the issues rooted in the dissolution of a marriage, but now she felt homeless and could not get her bearings well enough to function in the world. She found that

---

16 Elise Gould, *Wage inequality continued its 35-year rise in 2015* (Economic Policy Institute, 2016),https://www.epi.org/publication/wage-inequality-continued-its-35-year-rise-in-2015/.

retreating inside her new apartment protected her from stares and gratuitous greetings. She wondered how she would continue to keep up her image—that of a well-dressed, well-coiffed, high-end woman. She'd attained all that in her marriage, but before getting married, she'd never been able to live in that milieu. This was an emotional, material, and social loss—one that undeniably rocked her world. Instead of standing up to her new normal, she hid.

Linda knew that one day, she would have to emerge and face herself. She began by applying for jobs. The workplace was a good beginning where she could learn to develop her own identity and forfeit the one she had created as a country club wife. Fortunately, she found employment at a large company surprisingly fast, which was just what she needed to put her back in the game. As she mingled with coworkers who did not know her from her former social circle, she started to feel like the authentic Linda. She found that she looked forward to going to work each day. And while this life was very different from the life she had been living, this life wasn't so bad at all. In time, she regained her self-esteem, felt worthy again, and expanded in so many ways through self-actualization. She was no longer Mrs. Somebody. Instead, she had become a lovely, confident woman who could hold her own quite well.

Linda discovered that she was so much more than the trophy wife she had morphed into during her marriage. She had let her real self get caught up in a character she played to fit in and accommodate her husband. Once she became more self-aware and self-assured, she began to explore social and educational activities that might interest her and allow her to grow. Linda faced her fears and learned a great deal about herself in the process. Her growth and evolution were remarkable, and her happiness quotient rose considerably. Above all, her takeaway was that she had strengths that were valid and rewarding. With that awareness, she finally blossomed into her inner beauty.

Best Friend

"Sometimes the smallest things take up the most room in your heart"
— Winnie the Pooh
"An animal's eyes have the power to speak a great language"
— Martin Buber

Who of us who has been fortunate enough to have shared life with a pet has not equally known the searing pain of burying one or more furry buddy? At sign-on, you are surrendering yourself to a commitment for life. And with that, you will know abiding love and companionship. But as with any relationship, you risk unbearable loss when it ends.

When you grieve, you might tend to do so in silence. That pain is between you and the departed. Like any loss, it is an intimate event. It is not uncommon for others, especially those who have never had a pet, to try to mollify your feelings by emphasizing that "it was just an animal, not a person." This heartless lack of understanding can drive the griever further into silence.

Two out of every three American homes include a pet. Of the 393.3 million pets that live in the United States, most are dogs, cats, and fish.

- 85 million American homes (67 percent) include a pet.
- 95 percent of American pet owners consider their pets to be family members.
- 27 percent of pet owners are baby boomers. [17]

---

[17] "Pet Ownership Statistics," April 17, 2023, Spots.com website, "https://spots.com/pet-ownership-statistics/.

With all these pets comes so much love but also so much opportunity for pain. Together, we can weather these losses.

Betsy

One day, I received a call and heard a woman screaming on the other end. "I killed him!" she repeated over and over. She was sobbing between the screams, and it was terrifying. Naturally, I tried to calm her down and asked how I could help. More screaming and sobbing ensued, so I just kept speaking calmly in the hope that she would eventually quiet herself so I could ascertain what was going on. At that point, I didn't know whether I was speaking with an actual murderer or just a mentally unstable person, but I assumed that if she'd been referred to me, she was calling to deal with a loss.

And then it came!

"My dog, my precious dog. I killed him," she said.

"Why did you do that?" I asked quietly. Then she explained it was an accident. She and her dog had been very close. When she was driving home after work one day, her dog heard her coming up the street and escaped from the yard so he could greet her. The dog ran under her car as she drove down the driveway, and she drove over him.

I cannot imagine how that must have felt. But I heard her on the phone, and I knew she was truly shattered. She gave me an address, and I told her I would come over to be with her and help her make arrangements.

She was waiting for me on the front porch, and she looked like she had not stopped wailing since we had spoken. We sat together, and I held her hand and assured her that I would be with her until everything was taken care of, as the dog was still lying underneath her car. She was an older woman, likely in her seventies, yet the tenor of our conversation was one of mother and child. At that moment, her countenance was frail and unforgiving.

My goal was to get her inside her home so I could call animal control to pick up her dog. But she had something else in mind. She wanted him cremated so he would remain with her, albeit in an altered form. Her road was going to be challenging because I knew she would not let go very easily. She had no family, but I managed to persuade her to call a friend to stay the night with her.

We had many sessions together in which she alternated between hysterics and exhaustion, as you might imagine. Not only had she lost her beloved dog, but she had inadvertently caused his death. She was mired in self-blame and could not find a way to absolve herself of responsibility for the tragedy.

This takes time because, in her despair, she was irrational. Our goal was to move her to the rational, or, at the very least, a form of compromise. That served as a jumping point for her recovery from grief.

We kept in close touch in person and over the phone, and she told me that she slept with her dog's blanket and found that very comforting. For several weeks, we did the work she needed to do to acknowledge her sorrow and talk about her dog. We also discussed what he'd meant to her and what her life would look like going forward. One option was to get another dog when she was ready, while the second choice was to do the work to find closure with her pain and live her life without her buddy.

I sensed that she would choose the first option because she was very lonely and needed a companion. In time, that is exactly what she did. She did not simply substitute one dog for the other. But after some healing took place, she lovingly adopted another. She got an adorable rescue that was cuddly and playful and filled a void. It worked out well for her, and she no longer felt like a lonely senior citizen. Her new furry friend gave her purpose and love, and her life was renewed in a very special way.

The pandemic gnawed at our emotional balance. Could we survive in a state of isolation? And for how long? If you were like me and needed tactile stimulation, the remedy was opening your home to a pet. I adopted a cat. She needed a home, and I needed her as much. The affection that we have shared and are still sharing has brought a closeness that is singular in nature. It is an unspoken exchange of unconditional friendship and love. She keeps me company, she looks for me when it's dinnertime, she nuzzles next to me when I'm reading, and she claims her real estate on my lap. And I love it all!

'Til Death or Divorce

"There are no goodbyes for us.
Wherever you are, you will always be in my heart"
— Mahatma Gandhi

When you lose your spouse, it can turn your world into an amalgam of emotions—as grief mostly does. You might expect to have trouble sleeping as you reach for the body that used to sleep adjacent and find it isn't there. It is also possible that you are disinterested in visiting places that you associate with your partner, engaging in activities that trigger painful memories, and talking with friends you both shared. You are flying solo now.

"The psychological effects of losing a loved one can include intense sadness, feelings of emptiness, anger, guilt, anxiety, difficulty concentrating, loss of interest in activities, insomnia, a sense of meaninglessness in life, emotional numbness, and physical symptoms like fatigue and appetite changes, often manifesting as a form of depression depending on the severity and duration of grief. According to some experts, after losing a spouse, you journey through grief, growth, and transformation. This path might result in new relationships, new or renewed passions, and even better health." [18]

Liliana

One client put it this way: "So many losses, so little time."

Liliana came to me after her husband died. She was missing him terribly and struggling with her grief. A boomer—with all the plans she and her husband had made abruptly extinguished—was suddenly alone. So we began to explore.

Sure, she was sad to be widowed. And yes, she loved her husband very much. But what now? Her entire social life was wrapped around couples, not singles. She did not want to be the third wheel. Nor, it seemed, did anyone else want her to apply for that position.

Liliana, a woman in her early sixties, was not a fit for clubs and bars with the over-twenty-one set. So, how was she supposed to create a life outside her home? The obvious *go-to* was internet dating. Even though the thought was unappealing to her, it seemed that unless she was willing to give it a try, she had no chance of meeting men. And so, like a reluctant schoolgirl, she filled out her online profile and began her search. With a one-two punch, her hopes were immediately dashed when she was struck by the fact that none of the men her age were looking for women of the same age. Rather, they were seeking younger women. To her credit, she searched and searched, sent numerous emails to men her age, and barely had any takers. Discouraged and hopeless, she gave up.

We discussed other options: Join a book club, network at local cultural events, tell all her friends that she was open to meeting men, volunteer, join a gym or other type of exercise studio, or take up golf, tennis, or bridge. I suggested that maybe she wanted to get a job or start a small business, which would put her quite naturally in the company of others.

There is no question that geography can be a critical factor in the accessibility of opportunities. It might appear easier to meet people in larger cities, as they provide more avenues to engage in life. But that is not necessarily an absolute. Crowds of people can be intimidating, and breaking into social circles can be less forgiving. It is often much easier to get lost within a larger demographic and retreat into the safety of our own four walls. It is, of course, always possible to break those walls down by joining individual clubs, classes, and other social activities with a narrower, well-defined group of people with similar interests, motivations, and goals.

A small town might be less daunting, as there is often a more personal connection among residents, business owners, clergy, and vendors. Neighbors might reach out more, which helps bring about a stronger sense of community. It feels a bit homier. Unfortunately, some people can become agoraphobic with age, as it's easy to succumb to the routine of paralytic anxiety and angst.

Liliana felt incapacitated by her loss. Yet she knew she had to break through the paralysis to take her life back. Even though she was older in a youth-driven world, she knew intellectually that unless she faced her reluctance and trepidation, she would remain on the back burner with only her memories of discos and dating. This was not going to be easy for her. For more outgoing and adventurous people, the task might be a fun challenge and a kind of social exploration. Liliana, however, would have to grit her teeth, make several commitments to herself, and venture out into the big, scary world of the unknown.

And grit her teeth, she did. She decided to try the online dating world again, joined a popular service, and started dating. She confessed that she had no clue about the current dating protocol. It did not come naturally to her at all. But to her surprise, she finally met a man she clicked with. Her steps were tentative, but she felt a connection. So she let her guard down and decided to go for it. She felt cautiously optimistic, and the relationship was slowly growing.

Then, one day, he told her he was not happy and was moving on. Her heartbreak was palpable. She was devastated and felt foolish for thinking she could get back into the dating game. But after several sessions, she made a promise to me and herself to hang in there and keep trying. My belief in her was considerably stronger than her belief in herself. Yet she was a resilient and determined woman—someone I strongly believed would attract a new partner.

There is a beautiful ending to this story. Liliana did eventually meet a man who adored her, and they had a very healthy relationship that eventually led to marriage. As unattractive as online dating was to her, she'd kept her commitment and got lucky. Had it not been for her willingness to step outside her comfort zone, she would perhaps still be single and alone. Instead, she is enjoying her senior years with a loving partner.

The lesson here is clear. To be closed to meeting others is to deny yourself the possibility of a loving relationship. Liliana went for it despite her reluctance. When we lose those we love or ties are severed, we can still be open to forming new bonds. One is never too old to forge new and powerful connections, for as we age, we grow and gain a deeper understanding of ourselves and our needs each day. Once that growth occurs, we are more apt to know what steps to take and where to look to be fulfilled.

Losing a loved one is clearly a fragile space—one you might find yourself catapulted into. As a result, you might be physically incapacitated with new health concerns or emotionally wrung out with exaggerated feelings of abandonment. While we are all aware that death is an inevitable but definitely uninvited guest at any party, we still risk welcoming others into our hearts over a lifetime. We do this with the knowledge that one day, we will be without each other and will have to carry the torch alone. Among boomers seventy-five or older, 58 percent of women and 28 percent of men are widowed.[19]

At the beginning of the pandemic, we were forced to connect in a new way because we were not always willing or able to meet in person. However, many of us still go reluctantly to dating websites to meet people online. But it is not the same as capturing someone's countenance in person. If there is chemistry online, how can the relationship go forward without the human touch and capacity for physical closeness?

19 Benjamin Gurrentz and Yeris Mayol-Garcia, "Marriage, Divorce, Widowhood Remain Prevalent Among Older Populations," April 22, 2021, United States Census Bureau website, https://www.census.gov/library/stories/2021/04/love-and-loss-among-older-adults.html.

In 2022, the Federal Trade Commission reported that more than 70,000 people fell prey to romance scams, with a median loss of $4,400.[20] Some of the most common scams include asking for money or personal information.

Just be smart and do not blindly trust. It might feel discouraging to enter a relationship with so many boundaries, but it is critical to your safety and well-being. Hopefully, you will never need to be in a position of fear or have your safety or bank account at risk.

---

20 Emma Fletcher, "Romance scammers' favorite lies exposed," February 9, 2023, Federal Trade Commission website, https://www.ftc.gov/news-events/data-visualizations/data-spotlight/2023/02/romance-scammers-favorite-lies-exposed.

The Empty Space

I can think of no other loss as tragic as that of losing a child. While it is useless to quantify whose loss is worse, I remember all too well when I went to my grandmother's home to share the news that one of her sons had passed. He was my dad's brother, and my dad was paralyzed by the news. It took several minutes before she accepted what I was telling her as real, but how well I recall her reaction. As she wailed and questioned God, she asked why he went before her. She said that no parent should have to bury their child, and I had no argument.

We bring children into the world and do our best to keep them safe. But when our children become adults, we can no longer coddle and protect. And we certainly cannot insulate them from health problems, car accidents, or addiction.

The loss of an offspring of any age can be complicated. Sometimes, a surviving parent harbors the same guilt my grandma felt when she wondered, *Why not me?*

If you lose an adult child, you have probably developed an adult friendship with that child, so there is a double loss. Your dreams for your child might not have come close to being realized. If your child is young, you are equally suffering for the life they didn't get to live. Losing a child typically will result in losing a part of yourself, and it takes considerable strength to fight through it.

Brady

I met with a gentleman who had lost his son to bullets and warfare. Sadly, his son was in the wrong place at the wrong time and had no gang affiliation whatsoever. He was studying at a good school and planned on becoming an engineer.

Brady sat with me, and the tears flowed continuously as he begged me for answers. No amount of empathy that I had for this man could give him the answers he so desperately sought. My role was to help free him from his pain. Thankfully, he was willing to do the work. It always breaks my heart to see people suffer, but this man felt that his only son had been his entire life. With his son gone, he had no reason to live. This is not an uncommon initial reaction to the loss of a child.

As he spoke of his son, I could see his pride gleaming bright. So I encouraged him to just keep talking. One of the more interesting aspects of his grief was that he didn't know who he was now that he wasn't a father anymore. He believed he had lost his relevancy in the world because so much of his energy had been focused on his son and his son's accomplishments. Brady had identified so strongly with being a father. While certainly not old, he felt lost without his son and could not find his footing. His son, he told me, had kept him in the game. With all the civil unrest in the country, he felt like he did not know where he fit anymore. He was frightened. Ultimately, we thought that one way to honor his son would be to get involved in a civil rights movement or organization.

I am happy to report that after we finished our work together, he did just that. He is now finding his involvement and goal toward creating equity to be very fulfilling and is hopefully making some sense of his son's death.

It's never too late to engage in important movements. Perhaps, as boomers, we can battle the feeling of losing relevance by reinserting ourselves into the narrative of political and social change.

Maria

"My father was a scientist, Mom was a homemaker, and I was a pregnant sixteen-year-old."

And that's how our grief work began. Maria was in her sixties when we began working together to address unresolved grief and guilt that she'd carried for decades.

"I brought unthinkable shame to my family, and I really don't think they ever recovered. I had sex one time with my eighteen-year-old boyfriend and got caught in that dreaded place of premature motherhood. I tried to hide it while considering what to do. My thoughts were neither judicious nor logical, but it was my ballooning belly that soon betrayed me. I was, for the most part, still a child, playing a grown-up game.

There wasn't much of a discussion. My parents did not believe in abortion, and there was no chance of me becoming a teen mom. Off I went to another state to a home for unwed moms, sent there alone and terrified. I hid out most of the time but gradually interacted with the other girls. All of us were there connecting with one another as our bellies grew. One by one, the girls left, holding tiny, crying bundles and reassuring us that the whole experience wasn't so awful.

Then, suddenly and with little warning, it was my turn. It took a long time, but eventually, my severe pain morphed into a crying, minuscule infant who was placed on my chest. My parents were called, and they drove over the state line to reach me. There was no rejoicing, no identifying with a grandchild, no staring lovingly through the nursery window. It was all business.

The adoptive parents were called. As they examined the baby, I barely noticed their joyful tears. I was sedated and received an IV for energy.

And just like that, a week later, I was sitting in class, having returned from my "holiday.""

———————————◆◆———————————

I knew several girls who got caught up in the fray and were ill-equipped to make educated decisions or even stop to think about a decision. I am, of course, referring to the girls who got pregnant, especially before 1960—the year the pill was introduced.

Girls had sex, girls got pregnant, and girls had abortions. Abortions were illegal. And yes, the stories you have heard were true. Maybe you experienced it yourself. These stories ran the gamut from kitchen tables with wire hangers to the back of a storefront after hours, with procedures sometimes performed by a medical professional but more often not. Many girls died; some were more fortunate. Of those who survived, a great many were rendered sterile. Very young girls with hopes of one day marrying and having a family were butchered in back alleys. There were also the young girls from "good" families who were sent away to have their babies, only to have their families force them against their will to put those babies up for adoption.

This is a loss that must be grieved. I don't care how old you are now. The experience is traumatic and leaves a mark somewhere deep inside you. For many women who were the victims of illegal, ill-advised abortions, this was not necessarily the end of maternal dreams. During the sixties, in particular, adoption gained momentum, and women became mothers to babies who were waiting for a home. I feel certain that for each of you who has been blessed with the experience of being an adoptive mother, you cannot imagine life being any other way.

———————————◆◆———————————

Phoebe

Phoebe told me she had never recovered emotionally from her abortion in the seventies. Single, scared, alone, and not sure which hookup had made her pregnant, she'd known she was on a bit of a collision course. But it was one she had to steer by herself. Not feeling like she could tell anyone, she began the demoralizing process of finding a woman's clinic, making her appointment, and showing up by herself on the appointed day—all in preparation for the removal of a fetus from her body. In her case, the procedure was followed by an overnight stay.

The deed was done, and she dealt silently with the cramping and discomfort that followed. Released with no instructions, Phoebe went home and carried on with her routine.

While visiting with a friend a few days later, she experienced sudden, increased pain. Within minutes, she looked down and saw she was sitting in a pool of blood. Perplexed and frightened, she contacted the clinic, and they told her to return. When they examined her, they informed her that part of the fetus was still inside but that they would have to do the next procedure without an anesthetic unless she wanted to personally cover the significant cost. She was not in a financial position to foot the bill, so she opted to have them perform the procedure anyway, which proved to feel like nothing short of torture.

Phoebe's experience, as horrifying as it was, was not as consequential as it might have been. Thousands of young women died from procedures performed by hacks who had no medical training at all. Yet it was tragic, and she claims the experience still haunts her today. She never did become a mother; whatever was done to her left her sterile and filled with grief, guilt, remorse, and shame. Phoebe is now seventy-one years old. She has not done any grief work to deal with her feelings and is just now beginning to address them.

Illegal abortions were far from uncommon back then, and the consequences of such restrictions on women's bodies were serious. Studies have estimated that the number of illegal or self-induced abortions in the 1950s and 1960s ranged from 200,000 to 1.2 million per year. In many cases, these abortions resulted in hospitalization and, in some tragic cases, death. Even in 1970, when abortion was legal in some states, it was simply inaccessible for many due to geographic location or personal circumstances. In 1972 alone, over 130,000 women had illegal or self-induced abortions. Thirty-nine of these women died.[21]

Roe v. Wade was decided in 1973 in response to the plethora of victims of nonmedical, dangerous abortions that resulted in way too many women losing their lives. It would seem logical that history would inform present-day thinking when it comes to abortion and the opposition to it. For some, it has been incredibly empowering and rewarding to see so many women lay claim to their own bodies. Each step toward equality must also remind us of a time not so long ago when an unintended pregnancy could have meant severe bodily harm or even a death sentence. Yet here we are, witnessing history repeating itself with the overturning of *Roe v. Wade*. It is unthinkable that we have regressed this far.

Samantha

A woman called me sounding in full despair mode. "I need to see you," she said.

"What's going on?" I asked.

She blurted out that she had lost her daughter.

"How awful for you," I responded. "How old was she, and what happened?"

21 Rachel Benson Gold, "Lessons from Before Roe: Will Past be Prologue?" *Guttmacher Policy Review* 6 no. 1 (2003): https://www.guttmacher.org/gpr/2003/03/lessons-roe-will-past-be-prologue.

"She is thirteen, and I don't know what happened," she replied.

"You don't know how she died?"

"Oh, she is very much alive, but I lost her."

At that point, we made an appointment.

Samantha arrived looking just as worn down as she sounded on the phone. This is her story of loss:

"My daughter and I had an unusually close relationship. She was happy and loving, and she brought endless joy into my life. Wherever we went together, she attracted people from the time she was an infant. She just had that incredible charisma. I had always played with dolls, hoping one day I would have a real-life doll of my own to play with, and she delivered. We shared so many wonderful experiences, and play with dolls we did. All of it. All that stuff you do with a daughter: making doll's clothes, trying different hairstyles, shopping, dancing, baking cookies, dress-up. She was always my sidekick. Until she disappeared."

I was shocked and horrified to learn that her daughter was missing. "How did she disappear?" I asked.

"It was gradual, I guess, but I first saw signs when she was twelve. She started retreating from me. When she returned after school each day, she went straight to her room and shut the door. She shut me out of her life. I couldn't understand and still can't. What did I do? I was always good to her and with her. I am grieving so much that it is painful. And I can't find a way to get her back. I miss her and what we always had together. Please help me. Find a way to reunite us. I cannot lose her. I'm spiraling downward. Please, please help me."

At this point, I realized that when Samantha said her daughter had disappeared, she meant that she had disappeared from her mother emotionally, not physically. I was relieved to learn that the daughter was safe. But now my focus was on this mother's anguish and not a "missing" daughter.

The urgency in her voice was concerning. I felt confident that I could help. She needed to stop the self-blame and be open to learning about healthy individuation in a child. Her daughter's need to separate from her mother was right on point for her age. In talking more with Samantha, I realized that her daughter's identity was very much wrapped up in her mother as a role model. In fact, the previous year, Samantha saw some signs from her daughter that she was exploring her sense of self. This is a very critical and healthy part of development that Samantha's daughter was probing, and she needed to do it on her own.

Still, it was a very painful process for Samantha. She was accustomed to being in control.

It took many sessions for her to settle down and trust me. She still held on to feelings of remorse and guilt that her daughter's ephemeral pulling away was something she had caused. In time, she had accepted this "crazy" notion that her daughter somehow had to become her own person in order to return to her mother.

It did not happen overnight, and the separation lasted most of the daughter's fourteenth year, and there were sporadic periods of rebellion. Samantha kept up with our grief work throughout, growing stronger and more understanding of the dynamic of their relationship. Her daughter learned that she could assert herself into the process without the need to test her mom at every turn. They had finally reached a state of equipoise.

Woman/Child

Come dance with me, my little one
Rest in my arms once more
Let us embrace my little one
Safe and warm as before

Can we preserve the oneness we shared
When through my cord we were tied
The ultimate journey for which we prepared
It knew nothing of ego or pride

How you struggled to first see light
As you descended my womb to travel
And how we labored throughout the night
To reach morning and then to unravel

Walk with me my precious jewel
Let me feel what you hold inside
And use what I offer as your tool
There is no need to withdraw or hide

Your presence is rich—determined and strong
Your beauty is making its claim
You have what you need to bring you along
I merely gave you your name

We are the same—I have more years
Our plight is of one connection
We are the same—you have more fears
We are moving in one direction

You are like me—conscious and knowing
Filled with vision brand new
I am like you—learning and growing
Woman/child—today is for you

— Susan Dean

Balancing Act

I don't mean to imply that many of us are not still living viable, involved lives without sufficient savings for retirement. But for the vast number of boomers who were not able to put enough money away, are not ready to retire, and yet cannot find employment, it is a losing proposition. As of 2023, we are facing a huge retirement crisis. Health care costs are soaring, and there is too little retirement income due to price inflation.

A new report finds that a large portion (40 percent) of older Americans rely only on Social Security, and a small percentage of older Americans (7 percent) receive income from Social Security, a defined benefit pension, and a defined contribution account. Retirement income from these three sources is widely considered to be the ideal situation to ensure retirement security, particularly for the middle class. Retirees with these three sources of income are far less likely to face poverty and economic strain.[22] The COVID-19 crisis further exacerbated this already serious issue. Countless members of those fifty-six to sixty-five lost their jobs due to the pandemic and were far less likely to gain employment again when the pandemic was over. As older boomers age, they become more vulnerable to the disease. These

22 *Examining the Nest Egg: The Sources of Retirement Income for Older Americans* (National Institute on Retirement Security, 2020), chrome-extension://efaidnbmnnnibpcajpcglclefindmkaj/https://www.nirsonline.org/wp-content/uploads/2020/01/Examining-the-Nest-Egg-Final-1.pdf.

Americans have had to leave their jobs to prioritize their health and safety. This situation put many boomers into retirement earlier than they originally expected, further derailing their plans.

Visual Capitalist reported, "In 1989, the top 1% held 22.8% of total U.S. net worth. As of 2024, this share has surged to 30.8%. Although this figure has hovered close to 30% over the last decade, the overall rise underscores the growing concentration of wealth at the very top. While the top 1% has expanded its grip on wealth, the bottom 50% (1st to 50th wealth percentiles) has seen its share shrink. In 1989, the bottom 50% held 3.5% of total U.S. net worth. Today, that figure has dropped to just 2.8%, reflecting widening wealth inequality within the country."[23]

Claire

Claire came to see me when she was struggling with her loss of work as a professional dancer. She still had chops, but there were no gigs for her. Hardly the age of a chorus girl, she sometimes got booked in films in a minor role as a dancer, but she felt useless and demoralized and had no idea how to support herself. Some of us might remember the go-go dancers of the sixties and the discos of the seventies, where professional dancers were often mixed in with the amateur crowd. Claire did all of that to supplement her career as a ballerina. What chance did she have of finding employment as a dancer at sixty-four?

She could have anticipated that a career like hers would end one day and prepared herself by learning another skill. But we don't judge here. How many of us boomers thought our day of reckoning would ever arrive? We were too hip, too cool, and too in love with making the world a better place to think *light-years* ahead and consider a retirement strategy. We were just living the dream. The economy

23 Govind Bhutada, "Visualized: The 1%'s Share of U.S. Wealth Over Time (1989–2024)," February 8, 2025, Visual Capitalist website, https://www.visualcapitalist.com/visualized-the-1s-share-of-u-s-wealth-over-time-1989-2024/.

was great, living was easy, and we had Woodstock. Many boomers didn't think they would even see their thirtieth birthdays, so the idea of thinking about turning sixty-five or seventy was not even in our collective consciousness. We lived by the slogan "You can't trust anyone over thirty."

But Claire was grieving the loss of her wonderful career and experiencing substantial depression and despair. We discussed her options. I didn't have a remedy for all that she had internalized, but I did come up with a way she could incorporate her talent with the ability to make money: I suggested that she start teaching dance classes. And, remarkably, her classes from inception were in demand, and she began to earn a nice income. Claire was amazed that she hadn't thought of that. In time, she even opened a dance school, and her despondency turned to elation. Now she had a purpose and a passion. She was fulfilled, earning money, and interacting with new people all the time. This change had given her a raison d'être, and she projected that in every way. No longer stuck in feelings of worthlessness, she had found her way. Claire also lived with greater gratitude for being a boomer survivor and not allowing anyone to tell her that her time had come and gone!

◆◆

We have had a lifetime of experience, both professionally and personally, and have so much to give. But all too often, we are ignored and devalued. Millennials grew up with computers and social media, giving them a clear edge over us older folks. However, the boomers cannot be discounted. While there might be a greater learning curve in tech jobs, that is not to say these skills cannot be learned and, depending on the person, sometimes learned quickly. Not every boomer can manifest a business like Claire was able to do with a nice degree of success, but there are several positions we can fill with more efficiency and common sense than a much younger person.

When I view the world as it is today—racing along at supersonic speed because of technology and the ability to connect with others from all over the world—the *me*-not-*us* mentality makes me more than a little sad. Some of what we launched still exists today: the importance of addressing environmental issues, the quest for racial and social justice, space travel, and alternative forms of artistic expression. Unfortunately, much like the counterculture movement of the sixties and seventies, today, we are still a nation divided by politics, damaged by the recreational use of psychotropic drugs, and questioning authority at every turn. While my assertion remains that the boomer generation changed the world, I know that many of us are suffering now that we are not living our best lives. It is so cliché but so true. Whether we overindulged in substances, did not invest enough financially for our future, or were so concerned with materialism that we overspent, it resulted in many boomers struggling to sustain day-to-day living. And I stand by my belief that if more doors were open to us, many would choose to work past the traditional retirement age if only we were given the opportunity and not looked upon as dinosaurs.

Did you prepare for your retirement? Some of you are receiving pensions or returns on your investments. Your house is paid off, your adult children are independent, your nest egg is fat, and life is good. There might be a tendency to keep your belt tightened because you have become habituated to a lifetime of saving. None of us knows when our time will be up, so we might be reluctant to spend what we have for fear we will outlive our money. But for the vast majority of boomers who are floundering, life is very challenging. We lived large in a booming economy. We were brought up with a workaholic mentality, and for many, this was the unquestionable road to travel. For some, however, the drugs, sex, and rock-and-roll culture was pervasive and dictated new possibilities. Men especially rebuked the idea of donning a suit and tie after feeling the freedom of tie-dye and jeans. Why become an accountant when you prefer to play guitar? Why be a teacher when you can create pop art?

This breeziness came back to bite us with the realization that there was only one Jimi Hendrix and only one Andy Warhol, which meant most people could not earn a living *doing their thing.* Of course, some did work in the arts or less conventional positions, such as teaching meditation or yoga. Still, many of us went on to jobs and traditional professions. Yet some could not see the long road ahead. Saving for retirement was not on all our minds in the carefree days of pet rocks and bell-bottoms. Of course, with life expectancy expanding, what was good for prior generations no longer works for us. Many are cashing in their life insurance policies to have money to live on, while reverse mortgages have become increasingly popular, allowing people to stay in their homes without the fear of being homeless.

A fair number of boomers have ended up on skid row due to alcohol and drug use or mismanagement of funds. Now, as older citizens, they see no way out. The homeless problem in this country has become so extreme that increasing numbers of boomers are living with their adult children. Each state is trying to assess how it can accommodate the tens of thousands who need housing, but it is no easy task, and it relegates us to a predicament that is both tragic and untenable. Homeless boomers just keep increasing, and these are often not people who are receiving Social Security benefits or pensions of any kind.

When the Body Says No

Boomers of all ages, particularly the older ones, are confronting many changes to health. We have developed diseases we did not have in our youth. We take drugs not for fun but out of medical necessity. But always remember, we're still here! We made it this far, so we need to keep on struttin' our stuff and recoup our greatness.

There's no doubt that our health changes as we age. From serious issues to minor annoyances, we're probably all experiencing something different about how we feel and how our bodies perform. Health challenges are real, and they can be serious. They can also come with grief, struggle, and worry. No one will dispute that. But, regardless of where you fall on that continuum, it's important to not let health challenges consume you and become your sole focus. For too many seniors, health—symptoms, doctor visits, procedures, medications, and treatments—becomes the focal point of every conversation.

And that's not good for our health!

As much as you can, find other topics of conversation. Look for other things that interest you. Talk with your adult children about your grandchildren. Ask about your friends' hobbies. Discuss current events. And there are always sports to follow. Show your family, your friends, and the world that you're more than a collection of diagnoses. Thinking about something other than your health—at least some of the time—is healthy.

And if forgetfulness is troubling you, know that you're not alone. Memory lapses are a part of the aging process. Although Alzheimer's and other forms of dementia are a very real concern for us, not every instance of forgetfulness is a symptom! When a name or date slips your mind, don't immediately assume that you're sliding into dementia. It could easily be just a normal part of aging. If you have concerns about serious conditions, of course—you should see your doctor. But try not to borrow trouble, worry, and despair for yourself by immediately assuming the worst.

Alex

Alex returned from the war in Afghanistan with only one arm. When we met, he told me he was in desperate need of counseling. He was more sad than angry, although I am certain he went through many stages of feelings before our meeting. Working with him was challenging because, at times, I felt helpless to comfort him. But that was not my role. We needed to forge a path toward wellness, and he needed to believe he could lead a reasonably normal life with a prosthetic arm. Together, we grieved over the loss of his arm and ultimately reached a state of completion with his loss. He grew stronger mentally and gained confidence in knowing he had options available that would assist him on his journey back to health.

In time, he became more optimistic about his life and decided to study law. Alex admitted to being distracted at times, which made studying more challenging. But he was determined to ditch the self-pity and make a new life—one that was both meaningful and rewarding. It took some falling down. But with enormous conviction, getting up was the only option. It was never easy, but with a lot of support from those who cared about his success, he did it. I often think his achievement was that much sweeter because it did not come easy.

Stella

Then there was Stella. She had experienced a serious heart attack, the leading cause of death for women.[24] She was grieving, but she was also angry—very angry—not because she had sustained damage to her heart but because she had previously experienced obvious symptoms, yet her voice had not been heard when she presented at the ER. The doctors were still dismissive in 2021, even though there have been numerous studies done on the subject of women having heart attacks and not receiving the care they need when they need it. How many years will it take for women to be accepted at their word and not disregarded as overreactive and highly emotional drama queens?

Ultimately, she got the needed care. But when we first met, she was clearly grieving over her experience and the trauma it created more than the physical and medical issue of a heart attack. Stella made many improvements in her life by changing her diet, exercising more, and living with greater intention.

It has long been understood that heart disease looks different in women from how it looks in men. Women have a greater burden because they are historically not taken seriously at ERs when presenting with symptoms, as was the case with Stella. If you are known to have a genetic predisposition for heart disease, ask your doctor what you need to do to possibly avert what others in your family have experienced. While it is important to respect and listen to your physician, it is equally important to listen to your own body and advocate for yourself if you feel in your gut that something isn't right.

---

24 "Lower Your Risk for the Number 1 Killer of Women," February 22, 2024, CDC website, https://www.cdc.gov/womens-health/features/heart-disease.html.

We know that in both genders, the same rules mostly apply as far as lifestyle mandates. According to the *Dietary Guidelines for Americans 2020–2025*, healthy eating includes fruits, vegetables, whole grains, and proteins.[25] Hydration is essential, as exercise is key for each of us, regardless of health conditions.

If asked, I think most boomers would single out health issues as one of the most challenging of all losses. I hear this endlessly from older clients who are depressed over failing health or are simply not enjoying the same feeling of well-being they took for granted in their younger years. There are many clichés, for good reason, that speak to the aging process and how it affects our health, but freedom from this grief can be found only in accepting the fact that such developments are both natural and inevitable in all of us. There is no easy fix, and none of us can predict what our bodies will contract or when our parts will be unforgiving.

Boomers are by no means the innovators of health crises, as every generation has gone and will go through the aging journey. But we are the ones currently experiencing a mixed bag of aging ailments that pose an inner struggle for many. Women lose their breasts, men lose their erections, and some use hearing aids, while others have trouble seeing. The Harleys have been parked permanently, along with the miniskirts. But here is the good news: Never before have we had access to so much medical information, innovation, advanced research, and technology. We might have felt our strongest in the Age of Aquarius, but we are still able to regain some of that vitality through myriad kinds of exercise, from tennis to swimming, and from Pilates to yoga, hiking, or just plain, old-fashioned walking. Staying active is key, and each of us must find our own path.

We know it is essential that we maintain a good diet—including high-fiber fruits, vegetables, and whole grains—and a minimum amount of meat and processed foods. But are you equally cognizant of the fact that you need to exercise your brain? If you don't use it to a greater capacity, your brain will likely get out of shape, just like your body would if not fed. Start doing puzzles, play word games, or

25   *Dietary   Guidelines   for   Americans   2020–2025*,   chrome-extension://
efaidnbmnnnibpcajpcglclefindmkaj/https://www.dietaryguidelines.gov/sites/default/
files/2020-12/Dietary_Guidelines_for_Americans_2020-2025.pdf.

try crossword or jigsaw puzzles. That will get you going. Practicing memory exercises is a great way to improve or maintain your brain health. Perhaps memorize the lyrics to a popular song, or write down your grocery list and try your best to recall the items on it when at the store. There are many games to play on your phone or computer with friends near and far. Research has shown that brain-training games can keep you sharp for as many as ten years longer.[26] If you have a phone, you can easily download applications with several game choices. It can be just as stimulating for your brain to learn a new hobby or challenge yourself to become proficient in a foreign language. Whether it's cooking, baking, golf, or playing a musical instrument you've always wanted to try, there is no shortage of activities that will keep your brain healthy and make your life more fun.

The point is that to maintain good health, you need to have a balance of good nutrition, ample sleep, sufficient movement, and social interaction.

---

26 "How Seniors Can Boost Brain Health," Seniors at Home, Jewish Family and Children's Services, 2021, seniorsathome.jfcs.org/seniors-can-boost-brain-health/.

Parents Get Older

Boomers are at an age when they're very likely to be dealing with aging and ailing parents. The average life expectancy of an American at birth has increased significantly in the past several decades. By 2060, life expectancy for the total American population is expected to increase by about six years, from 79.7 in 2017 to 85.6 in 2060.[27]

It has become more common fairly recently for boomers to move in with their adult children. Parents have outlived their money or might require care that a child can provide. This is not all dismal. In fact, I find it quite sweet, actually, providing everyone is in agreement. There is a lot to be said for an adult child, as well as grandchildren, reaping the benefits of living with the older generation. Much can be learned, and much can be given, each from and to the other. It creates a culture in the household that can be far richer than a typical parent-child family environment.

Kim and Ken, dear friends of mine, purchased a two-family home in San Francisco with their daughter and her husband. The benefits are extraordinary. The young working parents know that their parents

27 Lauren Medina, Shannon Sabo, and Jonathan Vespa, *Living Longer: Historical and Projected Life Expectancy in the United States, 1960 to 2060* (U.S. Department of Commerce, U.S. Census Bureau, 2020), chrome-extension://efaidnbmnnnibpcajpcglclefindmkaj/ https://www.census.gov/content/dam/Census/library/publications/2020/demo/p25-1145. pdf.

are just downstairs if an emergency or other needs arise. One day a week, they do not employ their nanny so the grandparents can watch the children, take them to school, and participate in all their activities with them. According to Kim, the young boys are constantly running downstairs to see them, which speaks volumes to how children relate to their older relations. And yet so many children grow up without spending much time with their grandparents for one reason or another, geography notwithstanding. They miss out on all the wisdom and love that only grandparents have time for and are happy to share.

Not all boomers or their children want to cozy up. As *The New York Times* reported in 2022, "More older Americans are living by themselves than ever before. That shift presents issues on housing, health care and personal finance. Nearly 26 million Americans 50 or older now live alone, up from 15 million in 2000. Older people have always been more likely than others to live by themselves, and now that age group—baby boomers and Gen Xers."[28]

Even if your parent doesn't live with you, you'll likely be researching care facilities, assisted living establishments, nursing homes, doctors, medication, and transportation. AARP is an exceptional resource, as are the many websites that walk you through the process. To learn more about choosing a nursing home and paying for care and to get information on different care organizations and a comprehensive nursing home checklist, visit the Centers for Medicare & Medicaid Services website to find guides on choosing nursing homes or other long-term support and services. I have included a few sources at the end of this book, along with information on acquiring care for loved ones.

Eighty-nine percent of seniors want to age in place—or grow older without having to move from their homes. And more than half (53 percent) are concerned about their ability to do so.

- Eighty-two percent of baby boomers fear their par
  ents will be mistreated in a nursing home, and 89
  percent fear their parents will be sad.

---

28 Dana Goldstein and Robert Gebeloff, "As Gen X and Boomers Age, They Confront Living Alone," *The New York Times*, November 27, 2022, https://www.nytimes.com/2022/11/27/us/living-alone-aging.htm.

- Seniors living at home are determined to maintain their independence, reporting that they require and receive limited support from their children or other caregivers.
- Sixty-three percent of boomers say they are providing some kind of help or support to their parents.
  - Over half say they also have children under age twenty-five.
  - Household maintenance (40 percent), trans portation (34 percent), medical issues (33 percent), help with financial decisions (28 percent), and financial support (19 percent) were the most frequent types of support boomers report providing.
  - Baby boomers with children are more likely than those without children to provide no financial assistance to their parents, including help with household maintenance, medical is sues, medication, and transportation.
  - Baby boomers without children are more likely than those with children to provide financial assistance to their parents, including purchasing or financial decisions and financial support.
  - Half of seniors are open to using new technologies to enable independence, including having sensors installed in their homes to monitor their health.
  - Baby boomers have not turned to technology to assist their aging parents. Only 14 percent have looked for solutions that would help them ensure their parents' health and safety.[29]

---

29 "Seniors Fear Loss of Independence, Nursing Homes More Than Death," Marketing Charts, July 9, 2013, www.marketingcharts.com/demographics-and-audiences/boomers-and-older-2343.

Parents Leave

If you were like me, you were probably unprepared for the dynamics of being an adult child of an aging or infirm parent. It did not occur to me to ask my parents questions about their predilections for their last days. Are you informed about your parents' wishes upon their deaths? It is critical to have conversations so you can understand their desires and directives so you don't find yourself suddenly clueless and confused as to how to proceed. As you will read in my story, I had two parents at death's door, yet we never discussed that possibility until the very end. Maybe I thought that if we didn't bring it to the fore, it would dissipate, and all would be well. Maybe I was just terrified.

Though I lost my parents in 1999, I think my experience is timeless. I want to share it because if there is even one valuable takeaway, it will have been worth it. This story is lengthy because it is personal. I lived it, felt it, and still remember every detail. There is no possibility of recreating another person's journey through grief as thoroughly as I can tell my own, so settle back and take note.

Full disclosure here: I am an empath. Judith Orloff, a doctor in Los Angeles and herself an empath, defines what it means this way: "Empaths have an extremely reactive neurological system. We don't have the same filters that other people have to block out stimulation. As a consequence, we absorb into our own bodies both the positive and stressful energies around us...we are super responders."[30] She goes on to further categorize differences among empaths. According to her rankings, I am an emotional empath in that I feel so deeply other people's sorrows, tragedies, and losses. That has abetted me professionally as a grief and loss specialist but has mostly been a burden throughout my lifetime.

I threw away my mother's hairnet in 2018. It was tough, disposing of something barely used, pink, and sweet-smelling. But then, what was the point of keeping it? What use would it ever be to me? Of course, usefulness was never the issue. The net spoke volumes about my mom—soft and fragrant. Wrapping up her hair at bedtime was her signature, one my dad would have preferred to have been signed by someone else. (He was never a fan.) Imagine going to bed each night with a beautiful woman whose head was wrapped in a pink mesh-like turban that was fastened tight with hair clips. And her young grandson—how frightened he was at the sight of it, crying, "Hat off!" at every sleepover. Oh, how we teased her about it. We teased her about so many things. I wish we hadn't. I wish we still could.

Recently, I was searching in my bathroom cabinet and found some medication belonging to my father with expiration dates of 1999. Why not just toss them? Did I need a reminder of Dad's pain? Was I so steeped in morbidity that I had to hold on to every chilling reminder of his final days? Medication certainly did not describe the man or give testimony to his life. In truth, his response to the proverbial "How are you, Dad?" was always "Grrreat. I'm great!"

Some thought my parents' marriage was the ultimate love story. So, like Romeo and Juliet, they were seen as lifelong lovers who left together. But I didn't think that. Why romanticize an unbearable loss? Was it to make things right for me? This was not about love. This was, more significantly, the end of love—the demise of a great love affair that left its mark so deeply embedded in my heart that I could not breathe.

---

30 Judith Orloff, *The Empath's Survival Guide: Life Strategies for Sensitive People* (Sounds True, 2018), 2.

On April 23, 1999, I watched my dad extend his hand to the angel of death, though he did so very reluctantly. A few weeks earlier, he was on the golf course, playing cards with friends, sitting on the porch overlooking the lake, listening to Sinatra and Basie, and taking care of my mother, the woman he called "my girl." He was so proud of their enduring relationship.

At Mother's surprise eightieth birthday party, he passionately recounted their first meeting, when he was fifteen and she was twelve. He was with his buddies, and a group of girls were clustered across the schoolyard where the boys stood. Dad looked across the way and saw *the most beautiful girl in the world.* She was dressed in an orange-and-brown dress that softly framed her slim, young body. *Who is this beauty? Does anyone know her name?* he wondered. Drawn to her, he approached the small group of young ladies, his eyes fixated on this gorgeous girl. They exchanged introductions. Lost in his teenage hormones and racing heart, and with a smile painted on his mouth, he looked at her and told himself, *I have just met my future wife.* Eight years later, his words would prove to be prophetic.

As Mom glanced back at her wedding photo at her party, she laughed and said, "I had quite an imagination, didn't I?" She was lovingly poking fun at the tall, gawky man of twenty-three who would ultimately become a very handsome and engaging presence. Mom was a bride at twenty. As Dad would tell and as was repeated throughout her lifetime, she was the most sought-after girl in their community. She was beautiful, popular, smart, from a good family, and fun-loving. She had a great sense of humor. What a gift! The humor, I mean. While she and I were living on opposite coasts and I wanted to know more about how she was doing with her chemotherapy, she sent me a newspaper photo of Kareem Abdul-Jabbar (bald-headed, of course) and said, "This is how I wear my hair now."

Ever since I'd left New York and moved to Los Angeles, I had retained our ritual of calling my parents every Sunday. If something real newsworthy came up, we might phone on another day, but we tended to save all the news for the weekly conversation.

The call came on a Monday night. I was surprised to hear my Dad's voice as he, trying to sound more casual than petrified, told me that Mom was in the hospital and had cancer. No frills, no beating around the bush, no sugarcoating. Just in the hospital with cancer.

My silence was thunderous. My brain would not compute what I was being told. I knew he would never say it if it weren't true, but no part of me believed one single word. It was not possible. Mom had never been ill, and there was no known cancer in her lineage. She had even stopped smoking decades before.

"Did you get a second opinion?" I asked. Doctors were often misdiagnosing. A swollen leg could mean lots of things.

No, he was certain. My uncle, Mom's youngest brother, was a doctor himself, and he had been consulted for answers to all the questions: How long does the *cure* take? What hospital? Is it the best hospital? What are visiting hours? How much pain?

My head was exploding. I was spinning. Racing between disbelief and shock and trying to figure out a game plan, I assured Dad that I would be on the next available flight.

"No," he said. "If you come now, Mom will get scared. Let's just leave things for now, just as they were. You know I will take care of her better than anyone."

"But Dad," I pleaded, "things are not as they were. Nothing is the same. Mommy has CANCER . . ." The *C* word. My mother had cancer. "I want to be there with you and her," I said. He asked me to wait. I obeyed.

While we were growing up, my brother was always getting into mischief, and I just sat quietly by. But my brother was always joking and making us laugh, which often got him a pass from punishment. Both my mother and father came from families that perpetuated fun and humor. How well I remember my paternal grandmother still telling slightly off-color jokes when she was a young ninety-five. And my maternal grandfather laughing until his eyes flooded with tears, a trait he passed along to my mom. Humor was the mantra of our family. My dad's mother reared seven children alone, having lost her husband when she was quite young. Yet she always seemed to have it all under control. When I was curious to know the secret to her longevity and all-around survival, she did not hesitate: "Look for the good in everyone and always have a sense of humor."

My mom was funny, very funny. But how would that humor help her now? She began chemotherapy, a procedure that would attack her healthy blood cells, render her bald, fill her body with poison, give her uncontrollable nausea that caused her to vomit, and keep her from the business of life. The laughter quickly faded. But not one time—not ever—did she exude bitterness, show any signs of self-pity, complain, or ask anything from anyone, least of all her children. She was, as she had always been, stoic and graceful, assuring us that all would be well once she *conquered* the disease.

There were many times when my long-distance move to California, which put me so far from my family, left me sad and lonely. How well I remember when my husband came home and told me that his company wanted him to relocate. The benefits would be outstanding. When I told my mother, with tears in my eyes, she replied with her usual altruism and courage, explaining that I must do what was best for my family. I also recall being at JFK airport and seeing my two-year-old daughter clutching my dad's arms as if she knew exactly what was happening. I felt right then that a lot of hearts were about to break. But it was always fun when my parents came out to California to visit. The heightened anticipation before their stays—during which my children would cling to them for two weeks—always provided a taste of what it would have been like if I had not left the East Coast.

But we managed. We did what so many families do. We phoned, visited, and sent cards, letters, and photos. (This predated cell phones and the internet.) But the hole was always there. My brother's family was expanding, our offspring were missing out on a lot of cousin time, and the annual trips back and forth were fully savored and cherished. I did not realize the extent to which my departure could have possibly impacted my parents until I became a grandmother. A week without seeing my children and grandchildren is unimaginable but a burden I have not had to bear. As I reflect on those years, I understand how brave and unselfish my parents were, never laying the proverbial guilt trip on me for moving so far away.

It would have seemed less shocking if the call had been to tell me that Dad had been hospitalized. He had heart problems and had suffered a coronary at fifty. It was something to be mindful of but difficult to be cognizant of, as he was a fit, athletic, very active man who was always on the go. Going for an early swim, perhaps playing a full eighteen holes around the course, volunteering here and there, chairing a committee, writing a column for a community paper, lending a helping hand—all this was simply a typical day in his life. Nothing stopped him, and it seemed as if nothing ever would. Now he was faced with the greatest challenge of his life—confronting my mom's illness and helping her get through it. No matter how many different ways he viewed this new chapter, it must have read like a Dickens script. But he was, as always, committed to a happy ending.

Outwardly, I have always met adversity with a fair amount of composure. With a compelling amount of calm and clarity, my response to a crisis is to move through it and do what must be done to find solutions. That said, I now had a great deal of trouble sleeping and eating. My inner self was anything but serene. There was nothing rational about this, but my body seemed to overpower my mind and have its way with me. I brought food to my lips, but my mouth did not open. My throat did not swallow. Reminding me of morning sickness, the very smell of food nauseated me. And sleep was out of the question. There was no escape. I ruminated all night long, daring Morpheus to approach. My subconscious stood guard at the door, preventing slumber from entering.

Appearing functional to onlookers, I continued to work and conduct my life responsibly. But inside, I sank further into an abyss that held me prisoner and fed my anxiety. The helplessness I felt assaulted me like a strangler waiting in the darkness. Dad gave me my admonition, but I wanted to be there with them, providing comfort, holding hands, and doing whatever I could to ease the burden of the enemy's attack. But I held back. To move forward would be to disrespect my father's wishes. So, I remained in Los Angeles, trying to breathe and trust that all would be well.

Learning about my mother's illness pushed me into a spiral of stress and fear; I was beginning to show signs of acute anxiety. Friends tried to calm me by reminding me that there was nothing I could do to intervene. It wasn't like a drug addiction. I couldn't hold a cancer intervention. Still, friends and family told me there was no point in stressing, but that felt condescending, even though I knew everyone had the best intentions. What is key, I believe, is to honor each and every person's behavior and reaction to grief. No matter how many people told me to calm down, think positively, eat, sleep, relax, and exercise, I was entitled to my own feelings, and I was not going to give them up. Some turn to food, substances, or sleep in times of distress. But I am not one of those persons.

Given my constraints, I still had to figure out a way to move through my process without crumbling into total despair. So, when Mom left the hospital, I called—not every day as I would have liked, but more than just Sundays. We talked about how she felt, her prognosis, the next doctor's appointment, and her limitations. Then she would try to assuage the angst she sensed in me. She reassured me that she would kick this thing, the chemo would rid her body of cancer, and she would be out to visit as soon as she was able to make the trip. Every conversation ended the same way—with us saying, "I love you," and tears silently sliding down my cheek.

My mother's illness became a way of life for me. The distance was a major factor in my inability to find peace with my growing anxiety. No doubt, had I been able to see my mother, provide solace, and spend time with her, I would have been better able to cope with her situation. But being so far away, alone with my imagination and mounting fear, left me compromised and unfocused. Though I managed to work, I was consumed by my desire to be with my mother.

No longer willing to let the miles separate us, I flew to the East Coast and began what would become an intensive search for answers. Who was the treating physician? What was the downside of chemotherapy? When could Mom travel? What were her restrictions? How long until she was *cured?*

I was as ignorant as I could be to the facts and consequences of non-Hodgkins lymphoma at that time, and my state of denial seemed to supersede my otherwise typically investigative mind. My obsession was wrapped around seeing my mother recover and resume a *normal* life. Being with her made a marked difference in my ability to get through the day, as I was occupied with helping her and Dad in any and every way I could. My father displayed a deep sense of relief when I arrived, no longer feeling he had to bear the burden alone.

In very short order, I learned about the treatments, medication, side effects, prognosis, suffering, and dread. With her usual fortitude, my mother accepted her plight not with a defeatist resignation but actually more like a believer. She, at least outwardly, went through her treatment with hope and trust that the outcome would be positive. Try as I could, I was unable to make sense of this disease and why it had paid her this unceremonious visit.

My father and I had a tradition of taking a walk after dinner, something I grew to anticipate each time I visited. With a consistent sense of wonder so typical of him, we would walk to the lake, watch the ducks, sit on the bank, and talk. Occasionally, he would stop our conversation to marvel at the size of a tree or the beauty of the sky. A true romantic, he found joy in so many things—and most of all, his family. How would he, after sixty years of marriage, survive this assault on "the girl of my dreams?" While much of my concern was for my mom and her well-being, I had considerable apprehension about Dad's ability to cope with her disease.

An athletic six-footer, he always walked faster than any of us, but his pace had slowed. "Do you notice that I'm not walking so fast anymore?" he asked. "I guess I'm getting old." I hardly thought of him as *old* at eighty-one, and slowing down physically was certainly no indication of trouble. It was just nature taking its course. But I noticed something else. He seemed to be hurting. It was not quite a limp, but his gait was a bit agitated. When questioned, he admitted there was some discomfort but said it was "small beans" compared to what Mom was enduring.

It was with a very heavy heart that I boarded the plane back to Los Angeles, feeling like I was abandoning my parents in their time of dire need. But they pushed me out—so typical of them—emphatic in their insistence that they had it under control. Ever the obedient child, albeit an adult child, I did what was asked of me and reluctantly took my leave. There was no doubt that my presence had eased some of their emotional and physical burdens. But at times, I sensed I might be intruding on their privacy. This was a very personal time during which feelings were very raw and senses out of whack. This mixed message was a source of great confusion for me. Did I make it better, or did they feel worse because I saw their vulnerability? My parents were proud and resilient people who had scaled many mountains in their lifetime, mostly landing on their feet. In their generation, children were often shielded from private matters, which is so unlike the openness of child-parent relationships of the generations to follow.

Once home, with a sharper vision of what life was like for my parents, I attempted to reclaim my routine. Phone calls to them became more frequent, but my worries were no less than before. In the wake of what seemed like a surreal life I was now living, I found myself mulling over the years lost to distance and busy schedules. *Why have I made so few trips back East?* I wondered. The children visited their grandparents every summer, but I much preferred to have my parents come to see me in California. Carefree days of shopping and lunching with Mom, going to jazz clubs and playing basketball with Dad, attending the theatre and concerts, making Sunday dinners, talking, laughing, crying, debating, sharing—this was the essence of family life. Since my move to the West Coast twenty-four years earlier, we'd been robbed of that ongoing exchange and had enjoyed only occasional glimpses.

What plagued me most, I suppose, was our physical separation. Reliant on information culled from phone conversations, I was left with only my frantic imagination. I felt that life was whirling around me, and I could not quite grab hold of it. Months passed, then the coveted pronouncement arrived: Mother was in remission. Cancer was gone.

I knew it. I just knew she would not be taken down. She was too healthy, too vital, too kind, too pretty.

Life would be good again. We made plans for my parents to visit, probably in the summer, when the air was warm and the flowers fragrant. There would be trips to the theatre, dinners at all the newest restaurants, visits with friends, strolls in the shops, and time spent gardening, cooking, reading, and being a family. Spirits were high; all of us were so grateful that the nightmare was over.

In a conversation one day, my daughter casually confided that my mom had expressed concern to her over my dad's health. Historically a man of great appetite, he was not eating well, and his back pain seemed to be getting worse. My silent reaction was cruel. I thought, *How dare he worry my mother when she is dealing with so much! Is he trying to get attention because he feels neglected?* While trying to reassure my daughter that her papa was fine, I began to explore the mental notes I had made along the way. I recalled that first walk I took with my father when my mom became ill and how he seemed compromised. But that was so long ago, and he certainly was eating just fine then. *No, I thought, he just cannot cope with my mother being sick, as she is his heart.* It was understandable. He was frightened. He needed some nurturing too. Upon further scrutiny, it occurred to me that my mother never mentioned that he was complaining, only that she had observed things. Still, I figured aches and pains were certainly appropriate at his age. And don't people eat less as they age? I convinced myself he was fine.

And now it was time to celebrate! My mother was turning eighty, and we decided to throw a surprise party for her. The matriarch of our family would receive the veneration due her, surrounded by her loved ones. It was such a happy time. Invitations went out, posters were designed, a toast was written, and menus were created. It was party time. My brother's family and mine convened outside my parents' house, armed with musical instruments and balloons. As the singing and playing began, my dad ran to the front door to investigate the ruckus, saw all of us gathered around, and called my mother immediately. We shouted, "Surprise!" as she hit the doorway. There were tears, shouts, and priceless expressions that I shall treasure always. I loved that moment. It was so full, so rich. We were all together—the family.

The next few days were like a weekend at summer camp. Lots of activities—eating, storytelling, playing sports, and, of course, laughing. This culminated with a wonderful party at an elegant restaurant, which was warm and spirited. Guests enjoyed themselves, dinner was lovely, music was lively, and tributes were moving. But I could see that Mother was not sure. Her body language was tentative. She chose not to dance with her dance partner of more than sixty years. I was watching as her mind questioned the night. Her composure seemed blunted by something palpable to me. Though I never verbalized this to her, I felt she thought we were all there to say goodbye. I still believe that. How frightened she must have been.

I wrote this toast for her, but my daughter read it aloud because I would have broken down, overcome by emotion.

A Happy Birthday Toast for My Mother

We are all here tonight because of an inspiration...
an inspiration we call wife, mother, sister, aunt, nan, great nan, and
friend...an inspiration to us all.

You have shown us about courage, set an example of dignity, cheered us with optimism, and floored us with your continued sense of humor. You have always met life's challenges with a positive attitude, conveying to us to do the same.

How proud we are to have such a beautiful presence as the matriarch of our wonderful family. How blessed we are to have been nurtured and fed by you, to have been entertained and motivated by you. Never a complaint, nor a chip on your shoulder, you have always made yourself available to share in all our burdens and all of our joys. Nothing was ever too much.

We honor you tonight, the leader of our gang, the glue that has made us all stick...we honor your eighty years being there for us, to provide each new generation with an opportunity to know you and share in your legacy.

Mother, you have our highest respect and admiration, and with that, you have our deepest love and gratitude for lighting our paths so brightly, and for giving us a wonderful reason to gather together to pay tribute to our hero.

We love you and may you stay forever young!

Once I was back home, the jubilance of the celebration quickly faded as I confronted the truth as I saw it: two lovers grappling with losing one another, afraid of what lay ahead and how to surmount that reality.

Driven by a heightened sense of terror and concern, I continued to propel myself through my process, not even attempting to pretend life was normal as I ineffectively tried to adjust to the changes. My years of regret over time not spent with my parents fueled my thoughts of relocating to be with them. The past was done, but I could certainly spend the next years doing what I could for and with them. Grappling with the idea of leaving my own family behind and joining my folks across the country soon gave way to a decision. My children would hopefully be around for many years, were independent, and were doing well. My mother and father were writing their final chapter.

Throughout this emotional ride, my children were, to a large degree, carrying a greater burden than I. My concern was for my parents; theirs was for me and their grandparents. Straining to spare them from my disquiet and soothe their own, I *instructed* them not to worry and *implored* them to relax. Though they never bought into my posturing, not for a minute, together, they bore the silent burden of watching over me without being entitled to intervene. Fearful that I was heading for a big, fat, giant crash, they did their best to effect a kind of hands-free vigil to oversee my well-being. This was not an easy task. By the way, my children are outstanding humans. I just had to say it.

The often tenuous nature of remission for cancer patients was relatively unknown to me. In some respects, it stuns me now that I was not more proactive in my research into the disease. I think I was just so caught up in the absolute horror of losing a parent that the fear cast a kind of paralysis through me, and that impeded any kind of discovery. So when the call came, it was much like an insidious monster preying on a child's sleep—haunting, disturbing, and terrifying.

It was back. The cancer was back. Mom was out of remission.

If life were truly perfect, we would all live our lives at the highest possible level, fulfilling our greatest potential and making every moment count. But human nature does not typically subscribe to that kind of perfection. We bleed, fret, worry, hurt, isolate, make mistakes, give away our power, judge, critique, and undermine possibilities for a near-perfect life. That is not to say we do this hourly, weekly, or even consciously. All of us have the capacity for joy, but life presents us with so many tests and challenges that, all too often, our struggles blur our perspective. Not once had I become complacent about my mother's condition, but I had truly believed she had *fully* recovered and life would go on in a modified but hopeful way. That is what I chose to embrace. It was the inextricable pact I had made with my adjusted sense of reality.

Given my penchant for surprises, I decided to visit them without advance notice and just showed up one morning while Dad was having breakfast. As he was sitting there, reading the sports page and eating his muffin with strawberry jam, his burden was not immediately visible. As I pushed open the front door, he turned to greet his surprise visitor. I am not certain who was more emotional. It was seemingly a draw. Thankfully, the unanticipated visit was met with a positive response. In fact, Dad seemed to fall into my arms as I hugged him and asked if I could join him for coffee. Mother was still sleeping, so we had a few moments to get up to speed on things.

What followed felt like a lifetime of recapitulation—a groundswell of memories colliding and exploding. As we sat together, just the two of us, I was at once transported on that lifelong magic carpet ride, recalling conversations, excursions, dances, sleigh rides, Yankees games, Knicks games, Giants games, night clubs, summer camp, driving lessons, stories, music, Shakespeare, poetry, birthdays, and bowling. Memories flooded my core, clung to my consciousness, and tugged at my heart.

After more than a cursory glance, I saw that Dad looked somewhat empty.

"Mom's not doing well, Suze," he said. "And I just can't live without her. I don't want to."

While I urged him silently to hold on, no words ever left my lips. What could I say to this man about his lifelong partner and the possibility that he'd have to go on without her? At that moment, I thought it condescending to try to convince him of the value of his own life, so I found myself honoring his sorrow. Hugging him, I let him know he would never be alone, that I would be there for him—not as a substitute but as a daughter. The strain surfaced as he began to process my words.

What parent wants to become a burden to a child? It is unthinkable, really. We all hope to grow old as gracefully and independently as possible. My mother made me promise that if she ever became incapable of caring for herself, I was to take her in the backyard and shoot her. I am quite certain I am not the only one who ever received that mandate. Though said with sly humor, the message packs an unrelenting punch. But with all of life's vicissitudes, we can hardly predict a definitive future, no matter how diligently we plan for it.

A week was spent debating the merits of in-home assistance—mostly housekeeping and cooking. Mother was categorically opposed, convincing me that she was entirely capable of keeping up with her chores. Her defiance only loosely veiled her apprehension about what would happen next. Her independence was at stake, and her grip on maintaining her role was being challenged. It was only years later that I understood the importance of keeping things as normal as possible. Out of concern, I was constantly telling her to rest and trying to persuade her to let me assume the domestic grunt work so she could preserve her energy. But unknowingly, I was denying her the right to feel like she was still a vital and productive force in her own household. There was so much to learn and so little time to study.

Without any particular map, I charted my way through the often difficult and harrowing terrain of doctor visits, food shopping and errands, cooking and laundry, and somewhat normal conversations. For the first time, however, there was a hint of mortality. Dad sat me down and discussed their will, and Mother encouraged me to take home some jewelry, a few of her special art pieces, and assorted relics from my childhood. Closing my ears and eyes, I assured them I had no interest in taking anything out of their home.

And as for that last will and testament, I felt we had many years to discuss the particulars. I was in absolute denial. Perhaps more than denial, I was unprepared for *how to be* and *what to say*. I could do anything that was required and see to the smallest of details, but I could not embrace the idea of losing her. Leaving them this time felt different from my past departures. Something felt more real yet surreal as well. Pushing reality far back into the corner of my mind, I spent my hours on the flight home making my plans.

The next months were spent in deep contemplation of the logistics and execution of my decision. I would move to Florida and be there for the two people who brought me into this world, support them in ways that I was unable to do from a distance, and advocate for them when their medical challenges confused and sabotaged them. No longer willing to acquiesce to their insistence that they were managing fine on their own, I plowed ahead with plans to leave my own life behind. Allowing myself a few months to get my personal business in order, I continued to speak with my parents frequently each week, never letting on that I would soon be joining them.

And then another call came . . . this time from my uncle. "You better get on the next plane," he said. "Your dad was just rushed to the hospital."

Oh, I knew it. His heart was broken and now under attack. In what seemed like five minutes, I packed four suitcases, locked my door, said goodbye to Los Angeles, raced to the airport, and was on my way.

I am still not sure how I survived the flight or the taxi ride to the hospital, but I was finally with my dad, and neither one of us was sure of anything. Tests were performed, results were in, and I was probing: "How bad was the heart attack, and will he need a bypass?"

Imagine my shock when I learned that his heart was not the issue. He had *cancer!* It had spread from his lung to his liver to his rib cage.

What? I thought. *This cannot be happening. No, this cannot be. No cancer on his side either.* He was the youngest of seven, and no one who had predeceased him had cancer. *What is going on here?* I wondered.

I left the hospital and raced to my mother, who was home, sick, worried, and hurting. And all I could offer was myself. I was unwilling to write an ending to their narratives. Not knowing what to say or promise or suggest, I would simply be a caregiver, a daughter, a lifeline, and a conduit. She stared at me in shock when she saw me with all four suitcases. I told her not to worry, that I would get my own place. But until then, I would stay with her and my dad. It is impossible to know what she was thinking, but I saw a woman who was definitely unsure of the next move.

And so, it was the beginning of the end. With Dad home from the hospital, I was living in chronic contradiction—vigilant and believing that the cure was just another chemo treatment away while despairing and bereft of any hope. It was dizzying. It was quiet. It was begging. It was rage. Most of all, it was terribly sad.

The two lovers of sixty-eight years did not know how to part, did not know what to say or how to be. And I was too caught up in the onerous moments to assist them in their process. In truth, I was not prepared for this moment. It never occurred to me when I was that little girl who did not want to ever think about losing a mommy or a daddy that I might lose them both and together.

But after I admitted them into the hospital for one last time, no longer thinking I had any tears left to shed, I kissed my dad goodbye as he told me to take good care of my mother.

Then, thirteen days later, my mom went to join her best friend.

My ranking in the family jumped from youngest to matriarch in two weeks. I morphed from an adult child of two parents to an orphan. Then I returned to their home and wept as I packed up two lives. And I silently fought with God, with their doctors, with their peers, with shopkeepers, with pedestrians, with anyone at all. I was angry at everyone.

That was a very dark time and caused great concern for my children. Yet, during their own very difficult grieving, they were selfless. To me, they were so gracious and loving, so giving and caring, so nurturing, and so very concerned for my well-being. I was holed up in my bedroom, and nothing could entice me out. I did not want to talk with anyone. I did not want to listen to everyone who tried to mollify my grief by telling me how romantic it was that they chose to leave together. How they were in a better place. How in time I would feel better. How I needed to take good care of myself because that is what they would have wanted for me.

At the age of six, I confided to my mom that I hoped I would die before her and my dad because I could not bear the sadness of losing them. She very patiently explained that this was not the natural order of things and that once they had lived their lives, I would still have a lot of life left in me. I did not care, and I told her so. The sadness of losing a parent is something that none of us wants to contemplate. It is indescribable, really, and nothing can obliterate the pain. Not substances, denial, or a change of venue. The hurt follows you, lives inside you, and manifests in immeasurable ways on a daily basis. It was not until I decided to take some action to recover from the pain of my loss that I first experienced some peace.

Grief—the big, fat *G* word. How unlike any other emotion I know. It is never talked about, really . . . just talked around with a little hustle and flow. Just as I was inept at watching them both fade from me, I really could not embrace this time with any logic or practicality.

After a few weeks, my brother told me I should *get out of the house* and *move on* with my life. I was longing to reminisce about our life with them, but he just rebuked me and told me he did not want to talk about them. *Did he love them less?* I wondered. *Is he not grieving?* I did not understand his attitude. He was back to work at his law practice and living his life while I was hiding out in my house, reliving every moment of my short stay with my parents.

Of course, we know that grieving comes in all sizes and shapes. The path that serves one person is not at all helpful to the next. It is so individual and so varied that there is no way we can judge what another is feeling. My brother was impatient with me and my suffering. There is no doubt he was grieving just as much and that he loved our parents just as much. But his way was to keep busy and go back to work. Mine was to isolate. Neither one was more valid. And until it happens, you do not know what your path will be. Just know that however you grieve, it is your grief. It is for you alone to determine how you will steer through it.

As with any challenge, the way we confront and handle each hurdle will determine how successfully and quickly we can move past it. Some of us are forced to return to work immediately, minimizing downtime for contemplation and lament. Others need to care for families. The toughest struggle might be for the person who has a lot of free time because there is little else to fill the void that accompanies loss.

You are likely to be—or have already been—at this grim junction where you are confronted with that feeling of immeasurable loss and significant pain regardless of whether your parent is no longer suffering. You are still very much in the game of life, and you will need to march down the bumpy and slippery road of grief, where rational thought defies real emotion. I urge you to look ahead.

Consider some practical preparation. If you have unfinished business with a parent, try finding your way back to closure. Do not be afraid to discuss their wishes when their time of need arrives. Burial in the ground or a vault? Or maybe cremation? Have they made their arrangements in advance, or will they leave that up to you? Do they have a will? A living trust? I was so terrified that my parents would die that it never occurred to me to ask any of those questions. It was only in the final days that I had any idea about plans they had made. And that was because they told me.

If you are fortunate enough to have some warning, sit down with your parent and thank them for specific things they did for you. Not every parent appears to have done much, but even in those circumstances, probe deeper. You will find they gave you something. They fed and clothed you or threw a ball around or introduced you to music or art. Maybe they taught you to cook or sew, tell a joke, make a bed. Did they send you to college or organize a wedding? There are so many things we can acknowledge with more gratitude that we often overlook.

Spend some time telling them what they meant to you as parents. How their guidance was motivational and inspirational. How they served as a role model for how you live your life and have taught your children and grandchildren to live theirs.

But what if you don't feel that way? What if you thought you had terrible parents? Maybe you often felt they should never have become parents because they were so bad at it. Look deeper. What were their childhoods like? Can you find it in your heart to let them know you forgive them for the abandonment, the alcoholism, the physical or emotional abuse? Can you accept that they had limitations when it came to parenting? Are you able to drop the grudge you have carried?

And ask questions. If I might stress anything that I feel to be so critical, it is the importance of asking your parents anything and everything you want to and should know. Not every parent is willing to disclose their personal stories to their children. But find out about your ancestry so you can pass it along to future generations. Ask about your parent's medical history so you can prepare yourself and your children for any genetic predisposition to disease.

There are some beautiful ways to preserve a parent's legacy. Make some time to record them speaking with you. There are preprinted cards for sale with hundreds of question ideas that you can use to elicit responses, or you can create your own. I also encourage you to do some reading. If your parent is ill, read about their disease so you can better understand what they are experiencing. Read books that discuss different schools of thought about the dying process. Some of you might read books that reflect your spiritual beliefs. If it is important to your parents, I urge you to learn about what your particular faith espouses regarding the dying process and whether any rituals should be followed. You might not care for yourself, but it is incumbent upon you to respect your parents' wishes. You're here because of them.

Myriad factors account for a person's behavior in response to a given situation. What seems critical is the response itself, how it manifests, and how it is then handled. Whether the news is bad or good, every one of us has a unique reaction to the same information; the differentiation might present with a cry, a buzzword, an activity, a mood, or an emotion. We are all wired and programmed in a way that is peculiar to each of us. How we function as individuals allows us to feel and experience life in our own customized way and not quite like that of a friend or even a family member.

My reaction to my parents' deaths was acute. Not everyone will respond to the extreme that I did. That is the burden I carry as an empath. Some people who have had fair or even adversarial relationships with their parents or are estranged might feel sad or cry. And that will be that, except perhaps for the memories. For me, it was almost a two-year-long battle with my senses and emotions. It was me unplugged, and I neither defend my response nor suggest it for others. Hopefully, each of you will understand that the day will come when a parent is near death, and a reasonable amount of preparation will soften the blow to some degree. By preparation, I mean that if you ask all the questions, chronicle important information, and know in advance about all their wishes for their final days, the experience will be much better.

Not easy. Just better.

The Fire Still Burns

Splendour in the Grass

*What though the radiance
which was once so bright
Be now, taken from my sight,
Though nothing can bring back the hour
Of splendour in the grass,
of glory in the flower,
We will grieve not, rather find
Strength in what remains behind;
In the primal sympathy
Which having been must ever be;
In the soothing thoughts that spring
Out of human suffering;
In the faith that looks through death,
In years that bring the philosophic mind.*

— William Wordsworth

While I have devoted Part I to some of the losses many of us have experienced, I believe Wordsworth was telling us to treasure our memories of youth and beauty because they brought us to where we are. The feelings they evoke are a part of you. They tell your individual story. But the point is to acknowledge your past, then move on and live life. There is much to be said about aging because as we progress in life, we tend toward the philosophic mind. This is not possible in our youth.

From there, go forward. All the good times are not ever lost. They have carried you for a lifetime. Without knowing the dark side, you would never recognize the radiance. And it is up to you to create new memories every day—memories filled with light, joy, and hope.

You are in a period of self-reflection, which is so very critical for your spiritual and intellectual growth.

II

Live

The Years Gone By

What does it matter?...Reminiscence and such,
Retrospect is only a word, though it can mean so much
When those you love breathe far from you
You conjure visions, both vivid and new
You relive moments, both tender and cold
Not knowing whether dreams can ever grow old.
And then why should moments become antique?
Moments can be captured time after time
Why should hours of emotion be forgotten, ever to search
for the new,
Things tossed aside make a character weak.
Be strong! Don't rule out the past
Pleasant or trying, this was, and is, and will be your life.
Your life and only you to live it.
Don't let adventure abate with the years
You're never too old to grasp and learn
You're old only when you no longer yearn
This yearning to live...to live and thrive,
And when that's gone, so are you!
Oh, your body might still exist
But your soul is gone forever
Gone...just as the life you threw away.
You murdered your soul, and a murderer
must lose her life.
Now you quiver at being called a murderer
You shudder at the penalties in store
Now and then you stop to think
Was I alone responsible for my life,

Didn't fate play a part?
Oh no, you are the sole curator of your life
The interior decorator of your body
Design not with fate in mind
Instead, harbor the responsibility alone
And then, when years have at last run out
Regret will not be felt by you
No, you will be pacified as you enter eternal peace
Remembering forever the years gone by.

— Susan Dean

Life in Fast-Forward

I wrote that when I was fifteen years old, and to this day, I am not quite sure where that insight came from. But it was in me, and I still believe the words are a viable depiction of how we can choose to live this sacred life. Fatalists no doubt would take issue with this kind of thinking about the choices and decisions we make and how they determine our path. It is also context for a religious discussion. I believe each decision we make moves us along on that chain-link fence of life. To assume that everything about one's existence is predetermined at birth leaves little room for judgment, creative thinking, spontaneity, decision-making, and choice.

Life is moving rapidly all around us. For the older boomers, it is particularly challenging, as we have fewer years left to reflect and adjust to the fast-moving train. The pandemic provoked us in ways we never anticipated. How could we ever have imagined that we would see the world population diminish as it did and that this global disease would hold us hostage in our own homes for an extended period of time? This is why it is particularly important to contemplate how we want to spend the next years. It is up to us individually to design the life we want to live and make it the very best years of our lives. We had some pretty good ones, so let's keep the momentum in flight.

We have come to believe that change is good. We have been told that with change comes growth. To remain unchanged is to be stagnant, to be undeveloped. So, why do we desperately cling to the familiar? Why is it so terribly important that life and the people we share a closeness with be predictable and reliable and present? Our intellect tells us that change is inevitable and people move on, but our emotions often keep us attached to the past or *forever-ness*.

The Way We Were

S o here we are. We have arrived! But who are we now? No longer the youth of our yesterdays and considerably less idealistic, we are still the original architects of the boomer cohort, many of us senior citizens. Somehow, that does not seem to fit. Seniors and boomers sound like two very different species. We are not young parents bringing new lives into the world, wondering if it makes sense in a time of war. Most of us are not just starting on our career paths, excited about where they will take us. We are certainly not introducing the concept of women's and gay rights, nor are we engaging in anti-war protests. We already did that.

I would suggest that we are seasoned adults who have lived lives of challenge, aspiration, disappointment, and jubilation. It is difficult to avoid feeling disillusioned, though. We had so many hopes and dreams for a new world—one we created, only to see it collapse on so many levels. We were witness to so many astonishing and now historical events in the sixties.

Allow me a bit of historical context. In 1961, during John F. Kennedy's presidency, there was the Bay of Pigs—a failed attempt to overthrow Fidel Castro in Cuba—and the creation of the Peace Corps to promote peace and friendship throughout the world. The 1962 Cuban Missile Crisis between the US and the Soviet Union provoked us to prepare for potential nuclear warfare, and James

Meredith, who became the first Black student at the University of Mississippi, said, "I can't fight alone," urging other Black people to join him in desegregating educational institutions. We lost John F. Kennedy in 1963 and his brother Robert and Dr. Martin Luther King in 1968 to senseless assassinations. *Mr. Roger's Neighborhood* debuted in 1968, followed by *Sesame Street* in 1969. In 1968, *Hair* opened on Broadway, featuring totally nude actors. I know because I was there opening night! The Super Bowl between the Green Bay Packers and the Kansas City Chiefs was in 1967. Popular songs were "Hey Jude" by The Beatles, "Bridge Over Troubled Water" by Art Garfunkel, "Let It Be" by Paul McCartney, "Me and Bobby McGee" by Kris Kristofferson, and "You've Got a Friend" by James Taylor.

There is no end to the list of groundbreaking changes we were privy to and implemented in those years. But the point is that we are now living in a whole new world—one that is very different but, in some ways, the same as the sixties. Some astrologers say we are back in the Age of Aquarius, but if we just recall the lyrics from the famous song from *Hair*, words such as *harmony, understanding, sympathy, trust,* and *peace* would quickly dispel that notion, as those are not descriptive of our times. But if those lyrics were instead viewed as a plea and a longing, we can see a parallel between the counterculture that existed then and the current environment. There is much political, economic, and social disparity, as highlighted in the anti-racist and LGBTQ+ coalitions. We, too, have been living in a time of war, and the #MeToo movement might be compared to the feminist revolution of the sixties.

As children of the forties and fifties after World War II, we saw substantial progress going forward in the early boomer years, and the assumption was that this trend would continue. We could not have anticipated the Vietnam War, which began in 1955, and all the dissension it brought with it. Many of us became disenchanted while others were overtly against the American government. We had high hopes for a better life, one in which social activism, much like we are seeing today, would have effected lasting change.

Where did it all go wrong? Perhaps we brought it on ourselves as we protested the Vietnam War, marched to end racial discrimination, and, as hippies, often frowned upon real jobs. And I don't speak with hyperbole when I claim that many of us were so obsessed with revolution, being changemakers, and being anti-ists, that we might have found ourselves descending into a great big rabbit hole, floundering to find our way out.

How do we live our lives now?

The Art of Enough

First, we must live in gratitude. We made it this far, and that is a feat. Regardless of whether you are in compromised health, alone, or struggling financially, please remember to be grateful. Living in gratitude goes a long way. Make the most of being here and really live your life. Remember when Ram Dass gently suggested to "Be Here Now Be Here"?

Find a purpose to get up each morning. After years of working or rearing children, now it is your time. What have you been waiting to do but were too occupied to find time for? Perhaps you never had a bucket list. Create one. There are infinite options for us now. It's time to seek them out.

Where is the line drawn in the sand preventing boomers from feeling like viable, hearty, accomplished, and worthy human beings? You know what you are made of, and only you know what you have to offer. This is your time. Visit with your younger self. What were you doing then that you haven't done in decades? Maybe you painted or sculpted. Did you build model airplanes, sew your own clothes, or play tennis? How long has it been since you danced or spent a day hiking up a mountain to take in breathtaking views? Remember when you had a picnic at a favorite lake or beach, took a ride on a roller coaster, or just sat in the park feeding breadcrumbs to pigeons?

There is no end to the possibilities, and that is clearly the most exciting part about living in our senior years. So often, clients have told me that they used to do this and they used to do that. I try to bring them back to those things they used to do and make the case that they still can, even if they have to modify.

We need to get out the broom and sweep away the used-to-be mentality. Living in the past will cheat you of the present and all those beautiful things you might enjoy in your later boomer years. No matter how resistant you might be to this truth, your time is growing shorter, and how you choose to live is your decision. In every way, age has seasoned you and hopefully allowed you to feel more confident in how you move through the world.

We are more willing to express ourselves, take certain actions without concern for judgment by others, and discern what is really important. We have spent enough hours stressing about things that were not worthy of our time.

This is a different time. It is our time. We know our time is not without certain limitations, but a lot of those limitations are self-imposed.

"Why do you stay in prison when the door is so wide open? Move outside the tangle of fear-thinking. The entrance door to the sanctuary is inside you"

— Attributed to Rumi

How many times have you said, "I can't do that at my age?" That can't mentality will guarantee failure—failure to dare, to experience, to achieve, to succeed, and to know the glory of accomplishment.

Why do we lose faith in ourselves as we age? In certain ways, we don't. We've had increased knowledge, longer lives, more trials . . . Yet we often insert the can't-do thinking into our lifestyles.

Stop! It serves no purpose. When you were a young adult, you were fearless. You jumped without trepidation over where you'd land. You are still that person. Jump now. It might just be transformative.

Rediscovering Passion and Possibility

C onsider the following people, who have made their mark in the Guinness Book of World Records:[31]

- Seiichi Sano, who has been recognized by Guinness World Records as the oldest surfer, started surfing at eighty.
- Jim Arrington, age ninety, became the world's oldest bodybuilder when he participated in a professional competition in 2022.
- In 2015, Hidekichi Miyazaki, at hundred and five, was the oldest competitive sprinter.
- In 2018, the oldest person to ride a zip wire or zip line was Jack Reynolds. He zipped to celebrate his hundred-and-sixth birthday.
- The oldest flying trapeze artist in 2018 was eighty-five-year-old Betty Goedhart. She did not become a flyer until she was seventy-eight.
- Johanna Quaas was ninety-eight when she was certified as the world's oldest gymnast in 2012.

---

31 The Guinness World Records website, https://www.guinnessworldrecords.com/.

- Anthony Mancinelli, in 2018, was still cutting men's hair five days a week at the age of one hundred and seven.
- In 2017, Tao Porchon-Lynch was named the oldest competitive ballroom dancer at ninety-eight.

"It is not true that people stop pursuing dreams because they are old, they grow old because they stop pursuing dreams"

— Gabriel García Márquez[32]

Any ideas yet? I defer to Confucius, who said, "Our greatest glory is not in never falling, but in rising every time we fall."

While not everyone would choose to do what the Guinness seniors have done, we can take away a very important lesson. You are never too old to make your mark on the world or fulfill a dream just for yourself. Some of us are indeed compromised. We might not enjoy the same health we did when we were younger. Boomers can list all the ways their lives have been affected by health issues, major or minor. We might not have the retirement savings we had hoped for. But too many of us get stuck in what was rather than be motivated by possibility.

"We cannot tell what may happen to us in this strange medley of life, but we can decide what happens to us—how we take it, what we do with it—and that is what really counts in the end"

— Joseph Fort Newton[33]

---

32 Gabriel García Márquez, *Memories of My Melancholy Whores* (Knopf, 2025).
33 "26+ Joseph Fort Newton Quotes And Sayings," Quoltr.com, updated April 29, 2024, https://quotlr.com/author/joseph-fort-newton.

Journeys of the Heart and Soul

Travel is probably one of the more common desires of boomers who can afford it. Some get motor homes, travel that way at their leisure, and go when and where they want. They have no schedules to follow or planes to catch. They are in control of their destinations. This often requires that they sell their stationary homes so they have the cash to do this, but a motor home serves as a home on wheels. For many, this is a very appealing idea, provided their itinerary does not include international travel.

For others who want to see the world, this might be the time to do it. Having no more work or family commitments frees them to do just what they want, when they want, and as they want. This might include visiting a variety of countries, each for two or three weeks at a time. Some of you might be able to tolerate a six-week adventure.

Again, there are no rules now and no one to report to but ourselves. We just need to do some planning and take the leap.

Graciela

Graciela was seventy when she took a long-anticipated trip to Peru with her husband. She spent a lot of time researching tourism there, from hotels to restaurants. But her lifelong dream was to climb Machu Picchu. Sadly, less than halfway into their adventure, Graciela tripped, fell, and broke her leg. Fortunately, she had the means to get medical attention and somehow managed to enjoy some of the sightseeing in a wheelchair. They had been hiking another less formidable area as a prelude to the big climb when this incident occurred. Had she been alone on the trail in a territory unfamiliar to her, she would have been in great peril. For this reason, I strongly advocate traveling with a companion for your safety and peace of mind. Not all travel destinations will have sophisticated medical facilities, especially when you're exploring developing nations.

◆◆

Travel provides so much more than just the opportunity to see new places, although the value of a spirit of adventure cannot be overstated. It often feels magical to stand in front of a monument or palace that you had seen only in photos. Now, there you are, within reach of your next photo op. How exciting to stand on ground that so many before you have traveled but that you have merely read about in books and studied in school. Climbing the Great Wall of China or floating in the Dead Sea in Israel can feel stunning—at times, dreamlike.

Travel presents many more rich opportunities, and one of them is meeting new people, whether on a tour or in a cafe. Fellow travelers can give tips on spots they have already been to that you have yet to go to. Or maybe they tell you about their hometown, which you might have contemplated visiting. If you are open and willing to engage with others, you will find your experience exponentially maximized.

There is little point in traveling if you do not avail yourself of the new sounds, tastes, and smells of each location. And of the people.

If you are single, you typically have a slightly greater challenge traveling than those who are partnered. That challenge runs deep for many people throughout the senior years. If you do not like traveling alone and do not have a traveling companion, you might look into the many singles' cruises and tours that are structured just for single people or specifically seniors. It might not appear ideal to some of you, while others will find it to be exactly what serves them best for their venture. Since all the others on these trips are single too, there is a strong likelihood that it will be a congenial environment. Perhaps some bonding will occur. Even if you don't make lasting friendships, you can at least dip into your bucket list of destinations without going it alone. Consideration must be given to traveling solo at an older age, as it has its risks. It is just not a good idea to roam around a foreign country by yourself if you are unfamiliar with the region and the culture. It is always best to be accompanied by someone when traveling anywhere, as we are more vulnerable when alone.

Ever since I saw a 1979 film called *Walkabout*, I have been fascinated with Aboriginal culture and, for a long time, had a lingering existential question about something relevant to the story. It had piqued my curiosity for decades, and I wanted to go to Australia one day to hopefully meet some Aboriginal people and see what they were about. Some years ago, I went on that journey. One of my stops was Ayers Rock in Alice Springs. While there, I tried communicating a little bit with an elderly Aboriginal woman who was sitting under a tree in the bush, making beautiful necklaces. The conversation was certainly not one of any depth because there was a language barrier, but smiles go a long way. Children were playing, and I had a lot more luck with them, as games are games in any language. It was a very special experience, but I was still not any closer to getting my question answered.

The next day, I decided to play tourist and went to a show of Aboriginal dancing and singing. It took place in an entertainment park. After the show, there were some other activities being offered. But instead, I just strolled around the grounds. While I was walking,

I came face-to-face with an Aboriginal man who looked at me with a big smile. So I smiled back, and he asked me where I was from. I told him I was from the States, and he wanted to know where, in particular. I told him California, and he asked me to be more specific. When he heard Los Angeles, he broke out in laughter, which I did not immediately understand. He asked me why I wanted to visit bush country, and I explained that I had seen this movie long ago and that something about it had always gnawed at me. I thought if I could meet an Aboriginal person who was familiar with the film, I might get authentic confirmation about what I thought to be true.

Again he smiled and asked me what movie I was referring to. When I told him, he smiled even more and said, "Oh, what's your question?" We continued to talk for quite a while, and he gave me the answer I had long been seeking. Although I'd had it all wrong, I was elated to get the truth. He explained that he was an actor and the producer of the musical I had just seen. All the performers were his nieces and nephews. I congratulated him on that and told him it was a lovely show and that it was worth flying all the way to Alice Springs to meet him so I could put my question to rest. He grinned some more. I thought I had just encountered an unusually cheerful man and was waiting to hear what he had to say next. He then told me almost reluctantly that I could have saved a lot of money had I stayed in Los Angeles because he and his ensemble had just returned from Hollywood, where he puts on a show every year for Australia Week in Los Angeles. At this point, we both laughed ourselves silly at the idea that we had crossed paths with each other by one week and that I had made the voyage primarily to get my answer. Australia proved to be a great destination, nonetheless.

He generously gave me more time and explained a little bit about the Aboriginal people and their lifestyle. Apparently, they are not comfortable sleeping indoors but prefer to sleep outside under the trees. He also told me with a little wink that I should beware because, at night, the men whistle at women walking by. Now, I am not talking about Aboriginal people who live in the city and are working professionals. When I was in Sydney, I recognized a fair number of them in business attire. If not for their distinct facial features, they would have looked like everyone else going about their day. But I was asking, in particular, about those who reside in the bush. The whole experience was magical and memorable. For me, these kinds of random encounters make traveling and life so rich and satisfying. A wonderful memory had been created.

Now, it is also true that some people prefer to stay in American hotels when traveling abroad and look for fellow Americans to talk with when in a country where they don't speak the language. If that provides a certain comfort level, by all means, go with it. All travel modes are equally acceptable. It just depends on what you are looking for and what you hope to get out of your journeys. Many people travel with their friends and, therefore, have their own ready-made group. So they don't feel the need to reach out. Friends enjoying a shared experience can be fun, especially on a cruise, where there is a lot of entertainment and food! There is no one way to do it.

The Gift We Become

Perhaps you are done with traveling and are thinking in another direction. What about starting a business? Does that sound out of reach? Wait! The first boomer cohort is in their late seventies now, and the younger ones are in their early sixties. Surely, you must recognize that others have accomplished much greater feats at your age. And some were quite a bit older, as pointed out in some of my references from the *Guinness Book of World Records*. Each day that you spend just contemplating your dream business is another day of inaction. Go back as far as your childhood. Was there something you dreamed of doing when you were all grown up? Maybe you can leverage that fantasy into something real today.

Perhaps you don't need the money. Do it for the pure joy of doing it, like when you were a child. Back then, you engaged in activities just because you enjoyed them without an agenda. Maybe you played ball or ice-skated on a lake when it was frozen over just because you could. You had no end game in mind.

I'm not suggesting that if you decide to start a business, you should do it without a business plan, an end goal, or a desire to grow your business and make money. Consider all your prospects. If you are a good baker, sell your cookies online and create income while doing something you enjoy. If you've always enjoyed woodworking, think about creating objects to sell, large or small. Artists, bring the canvases and clay out of storage; writers, start writing; and yogis, think about teaching an online class. There is no end to the possibilities if only you avail yourself of them. If you are good at speaking a foreign language, start a tutoring business for high school and college students who need extra help. If you know the inside of a computer intimately, start a troubleshooting business. Can you give piano lessons? You know what you can do, and only you know what it takes.

Where is your motivation? Has it faded with the years? Is it packed away in an old suitcase? Drag it out and give it a good shake, then tell yourself that you are ready to do this. You cannot afford to throw in the towel. There's so much left to do, see, and give. This is the kind of thing you had no time for when you were working full-time. Now is the time. Make it happen. Believe in yourself. Allocate a portion of your day to it, but save some time to play. Create the balance. I promise this will get your motor running. You might need a tune-up occasionally, but you will be ready to roll. Get back in the game and feel vital again, just like back in the day.

After much consideration, maybe you have decided that starting a business is not for you. That's okay. So now you might consider how you can put your assets to work in a less demanding way. Volunteer. Volunteer. Volunteer. Boomers have so much to offer to others, young and old. Perhaps art is your thing. Then you could become a docent at a museum. Do you love children? Be a Big Brother or Big Sister. Love books? Read to a child in an after-school program. You absolutely adore animals? Offer your time at a stable or a shelter or as a dog walker. Is theatre your interest? You can be a greeter, ticket taker, or usher and get to see productions for free.

"The purpose of life is to discover your gift. The work of life is to develop it. The meaning of life is to give your gift away"

— David Viscott[34]

---

34 David Viscott, *Finding Your Strength in Difficult Times: A Book of Meditations* (McGraw Hill, 1993).

We all have a responsibility to give back. Life has given us much, and we have much to share. Regardless of your financial health, you have other assets, and you can share them with those eager to learn. If you are in good physical condition and enjoy being by the sea, you can join one of the many organizations that clean up beaches. There is also a great need to pick up litter from the parks. Why not be adventurous? When a crisis hits a city, get in your car or on a plane and help rebuild homes. This is a win-win because you are supporting people in need and keeping yourself physically fit in the process.

Carlos

A client I saw a few years back was a strapping presence at seventy-one. But like so many others, he felt completely out of step. He had been married since he was twenty years old and was now widowed. As we dug deeper into his interests, he told me that he always liked doing things around the house and was considered very skilled. At first, he started doing favors for friends, so I suggested that he capitalize on that, use his skills for profit, become a professional Mr. Fix-It, and start his own business. That is exactly what he did. Now he is happier than he could have ever imagined and is in high demand. He still makes time for volunteer work, which is a credit to his character. But a little spending change on the side never hurts either.

◆◆

Hospitals are always in need of volunteers who perform a vast assortment of tasks, both administrative and on the patient floors.

Working with patients can be incredibly rewarding, if only to bring a smile to a sick person's face by offering a cookie or magazine. There are those in need of help walking around the halls when aides are unavailable. Sometimes, patients just crave conversation and companionship. It is so important to remember that not everyone has a family member or friend to show up and commiserate or encourage, and that is so fundamental to healing.

Some of you older female boomers might remember taking home economics in school and learning how to sew. If you've kept up with those skills, there are so many shelters, charities, and places of worship that would love to have donations of clothes you've sewn. Perhaps you can start a free class for young girls and boys interested in learning to sew or for contemporaries who would love to get back into sewing. How many of you have adult children who cannot even sew a button on a shirt? Maybe your class will inspire future designers.

Have you been lauded for your culinary skills? Countless meals have been cooked over the years, and yes, over the decades, you have intimately bonded with a cooktop and oven. Maybe you have happily retired your apron. Your mastery would not be wasted in a soup kitchen, serving meals to the homeless at Thanksgiving or distributing food to those in need on a more regular basis. If you are not entirely burned out and can manage an apple pie or a batch of chocolate chip cookies, your donations to nursing homes and homeless shelters would be a welcome addition. Schools are also looking for baked goods and casseroles to sell at their fundraising events. I like to drop off a treat or two at my local fire and police station as a way of letting them know they are appreciated.

Now, what about our future leaders, educators, changemakers, and influencers? We might be viewed as *old school* and not know how to build a website, but there can be no doubt that we have a plethora of life experiences and education to pass along to the generation that is just starting on their pursuits. How many of you have considered mentoring, either through an organization or for young persons you know through family or friends, so you can share your wealth of knowledge with them?

This is very different from tutoring. Some children either have little to no guidance at home or need an outside perspective that they find more relatable than the one they are receiving from their parents. This does not mean you would be a substitute. Rather, you would be more of an enhancement to bring awareness and enrichment to their lives. Some youngsters have never been to a museum, movie theatre, beach, or sporting event. Taking children on an outing of any kind that might be a new experience adds invaluably to their growth.

Do you love books? Volunteer at a local library and read to young children at story hour. Mentoring youth is just a wonderful thing to do, especially today, when so many households are headed by two working parents who barely have the time to read a book to their young ones at bedtime. Were you a great athlete in your younger days? Coach children at a local YMCA or in an after-school program at a community center. Or just give lessons to help kids improve their game. We underestimate our value as boomers and forget how much we can advance young lives.

These are just a few ideas to help you contemplate the notion and importance of volunteering. I am quite certain that as you peruse your strengths, you will come up with the right fit for you. If you find yourself without direction as to where or how to put your skills to work, AARP always has a list of organizations you can contact to take it to the next step. Places of worship are often in need of volunteers for a variety of things. Religious institutions can be a viable outlet for meeting like-minded peers. There are often activities offered, such as games, dances, lectures, classes, concerts, and other forms of entertainment. Senior community centers also extend similar kinds of events and classes.

What are some of the issues we are wrestling with the most? We are social beings. We are meant to engage with others. While I have suggested ways to stay active, it might sound counterintuitive as we are still somewhat challenged by COVID-19 and attendant viruses. This has been perhaps one of the biggest tests of our lifetime. Forced quarantine for the older population rendered so many of us fearful and lonely. Those without a significant other, family member, or roommate were therefore quarantined alone. Even today, when we order food and all our other essential items online, we are basically in communication only with our phone or computer. The virus just added another layer of frustration and provocation for our age group.

The Space Between Us

Certainly, statistics tell us that loneliness is too often front and center in a boomer's life. Then we were told to quarantine, wear a mask, and practice social distancing. People all too frequently resort to substances as a coping mechanism during times of crisis or from the despair of loneliness. Even before the COVID pandemic, public health experts were concerned about an epidemic of loneliness in the US. "Approximately half of US adults report experiencing loneliness," according to the 2023 report, "Our Epidemic of Loneliness and Isolation: The U.S. Surgeon General's Advisory on the Healing Effects of Social Connection and Community."[35]

For the 38.5 million Americans who live alone,[36] that implies there's no meaningful social contact at all, potentially for months on end. A report from the National Academies of Sciences, Engineering, and Medicine found that one-fourth of adults sixty-five and older considered themselves to be socially isolated. Many studies show how chronic loneliness has clear links to a long list of health problems, including dementia, depression, anxiety, self-harm, suicide, heart

---

35 *Our Epidemic of Loneliness and Isolation: The U.S. Surgeon General's Advisory on the Healing Effects of Social Connection and Community* (The Commissioned Corps of the U.S. Public Health Service, 2023), chrome-extension://efaidnbmnnnibpcajpcglclefindmkaj/https://www.hhs.gov/sites/default/files/surgeon-general-social-connection-advisory.pdf.
36 United States Census Bureau, "Nearly Two-Thirds of U.S. Households Are Family Households," news release, November 12, 2024.

conditions, stroke, and an earlier demise. People without social support also have lower chances of full recovery after a serious illness than people with a strong network.[37]

Many boomers are single and living on their own because they are either divorced or widowed. Some of us have children, and some have children who don't live nearby. There is epidemic loneliness and isolation among boomers of all ages. Social isolation and loneliness are serious yet underappreciated public health risks that affect a significant portion of the older adult population. Approximately 37 percent of Americans aged fifty to eighty experience loneliness, and 34 percent report being socially isolated. The good news: Improving your social connections is linked to increased longevity and better social, emotional, and physical well-being.[38]

An often overlooked factor of isolation is that older people do not have sufficient physical contact to keep them as healthy as they might be. We all need to be touched, caressed, hugged, and kissed. It is a human need. We were spoiled by the freedom with which we enjoyed all those things when we were making our mark in the world. Now we sit and wait for someone to come along and touch our hand and linger. Our memory goes back to our younger years, when we had it all, and it makes the void feel even more ubiquitous.

Baby boomers are aging alone more than any generation in US history, and the resulting loneliness is a looming public health threat. In 2022, there were 26 million Americans over fifty living alone. The Census Bureau expects the baby boomer population to reach 61.3 million by 2029 and that people over sixty-five will compose 20 percent of the country's population.[39]

In his advisory, US Surgeon General Vivek Murthy, M.D., warned that loneliness is far more than just a bad feeling—it is an epidemic that harms both individual and societal health. Social connection is

37 *Social Isolation and Loneliness in Older Adults* (National Academies of Sciences, Engineering, and Medicine, 2020).
38 LB, Gerlach, ES Solway, and PN Malani, "Social Isolation and Loneliness in Older Adults." *JAMA*. 2024;331(23):2058. doi:10.1001/jama.2024.3456.
39 "More Aging Baby Boomers Are Living Alone—How Do They Compare With Previous Generations?" *Forbes*, December 11, 2022, https://www.forbes.com/sites/qai/2022/12/11/more-aging-baby-boomers-are-living-alone---how-do-they-compare-with-previous-generations/.

"a fundamental human need, as essential to survival as food, water, and shelter," he said.[40]

Friends play an invaluable role in our lives. As the Beatles told us, we can't get by without our friends. But long before they came on the scene, perhaps one of my favorite quotes comes from Aristotle: "Without friends, no one would choose to live though he had all other goods."[41] We, as human beings, need our friendships. Nourish your relationships and let friends know that they are in your thoughts and in your heart. It goes a long way. Remember that while you might be leading a busy life with companionship, so many others are alone and floundering.

So, how do you keep going during periods of isolation? This is an entirely individual path. Some can occupy their days reading while others watch television shows and movies. Music lovers haul out their record albums and 45s, and others become reacquainted with their out-of-tune pianos. One ambitious friend with an enormous record collection told me he decided to use his time in quarantine to catalog all his music, which spans sixty years.

Ambition is worth noting here because so many of us are finding we are void of motivation. This is common, not only for those in a period of quarantine but also for those who are solo travelers. Why get dressed and comb your hair if no one will see you? Why not eat out of a can or frozen dinner package?

The answer is simple, really. You need to do it for yourself. You count.

Whether getting through a life-threatening global health crisis or living the life you have carved out, it is critical to remember that you matter. We all are painfully aware by now that a basket of happiness is unlikely to fall out of the sky to anoint us with good cheer. The pandemic presented us with a host of new feelings and thoughts that I am guessing might have otherwise slipped through the cracks. It was truly a time of reflection and, in many cases, I am confident,

---

40 *Our Epidemic of Loneliness and Isolation: The U.S. Surgeon General's Advisory on the Healing Effects of Social Connection and Community* (The Commissioned Corps of the U.S. Public Health Service, 2023), chrome-extension://efaidnbmnnnibpcajpcglclefindmkaj/https://www.hhs.gov/sites/default/files/surgeon-general-social-connection-advisory.pdf.
41 Aristotle, *Aristotle's Nicomachean Ethics*, trans. Robert C. Bartlett and Susan D. Collins (University of Chicago Press, 2012), 122.

regret. We were besieged by rules and regulations that were life-altering. Some of us are now part of the high-risk community just by being elderly. We might be in great health, but our age relegates us to a different category.

How many of you felt you did not have this time to forfeit? Has the clock been ticking louder? At the height of the pandemic, we didn't know when things would get back to normal or if they ever would in our lifetimes. We were saddened when we could not see our family, watch our grandchildren as they grew, visit with friends, and have fun outings. It was a time of high anxiety. We were following the stay-at-home guidelines, but then we turned on the television news programs, only to see the younger generation turn their noses up at authority and ditch their masks. After the first few months, we surpassed the death toll of the Vietnam War, the wars in Iraq and Afghanistan, and the 9/11 terrorist attacks, collectively. Can you imagine that? It is unimaginable, really.

Living Fully, Living Now

So now we are the senior demographic witnessing the youthful cohort buck the system. We're watching them act as though they are invincible through it all. Sound familiar? Surely, this is not payback, but it is a bit daunting to be at the other end of this dynamic. So many of us were feeling lonelier than we'd ever anticipated. We had to be safe, but we were longing for human contact. We felt vulnerable but were often on the verge of breaking the quarantine to visit a friend or two. Of course we were feeling that way. To live in isolation is so contrary to the way we are meant to live. We are social beings who need social interaction, engagement, agency, and a social network.

Unfortunately, there was no easy answer. Being alone and confined felt like being in prison. However, there is much to be said for confinement. I viewed it as an opportunity rather than an impediment. Think about all the projects you have resisted for years because there was always something else more appealing or pressing. What about now? Have you finished cleaning out all your closets? How about those boxes of photos? Are they organized by year, put in albums, or sent away to be digitized? Is all your paperwork for your children or next of kin in order?

There are infinite online courses to take, ranging from politics to graphic design. You can return to school and study anything at all.

Without being critiqued or graded, you are doing something very important. You are exercising your brain. It's no secret that as we age into the senior camp, we all experience varying degrees of cognitive decline, and we will have visual and auditory loss. How much so varies among us.

Research has shown that exercising the brain, whether by playing brain games or learning something new, strengthens the connections between brain cells and can actually delay symptoms of cognitive decline. While it is impossible to guarantee that this will prevent dementia or Alzheimer's, the research is promising in showing that our brains truly do grow physically stronger the more we engage them. And that keeps our minds working better for longer.[42] This is critical to retaining mental well-being throughout our aging years. You can learn a trade or study something that will provide a second career if that would be of interest to you. Seniors have never before had so many available options. These are not our parents' retirement years. We are a vibrant, vital, energetic, enthusiastic bunch. There is no stopping us. Look out, millennials and others. We're not going anywhere anytime soon, except forward!

We need to tap into our creativity and resourcefulness so we can sustain ourselves. Unlike during the pandemic, when we had many restrictions in place, we're now free. And we must be careful not to self-impose further constraints. Bust through and prevail as you know so well how to do. Your memory of days past can inform how you spend your time now if you are willing to let go. Live your life with a certain urgency each day. Don't let us down. Not now. Your tenacity and endurance are needed more than ever.

Perhaps you have a proclivity for fundraising or event planning. There are countless charitable foundations and organizations that are always looking for assistance. Try making a list of your interests and skill sets, then dig in to see where you would be a perfect fit. You might be surprised at what you uncover, see a whole other side of yourself, and discover your untapped usefulness. There is an outcry by a fair number of retired boomers who feel impotent in this fast-

---

42 Annie Stuart, "Brain Exercises and Dementia," November 27, 2022, WebMD website, https://www.webmd.com/alzheimers/preventing-dementia-brain-exercises#1-2.

forward world we live in. We, who were neither nursed on technology nor fed social media for breakfast, are grappling to stay current and vital.

Are you a retired teacher? Did you ever consider teaching a class at a local community college or senior center? You can share your lifetime of knowledge without being locked into a full-time commitment. There might be surprise gratification in getting a group together and speaking on a subject you know well. Maybe you weren't a teacher. Maybe your profession was law. You can create a seminar for first-year law students or undergraduates who want to enter the legal profession. Be innovative. Be an original. Imagine the unimaginable. You got this.

Have you ever had a hobby or thought about starting one? There's no time like the present, is there? Even if you don't know what hobby you would like to start, you can research others' hobbies. Maybe one of them will speak to you.

One of my friends was bored after he retired and started tracing his family roots. Now there is hardly a day when you won't find him working at it on the computer, and he gets so much pleasure from the treasures he unearths. Another boomer I know surfed in his younger days. Once retired, he decided to get out the board and give it a try. He has been surfing ever since. Nothing gives him the high that riding those waves does. It is also giving him a sense of community with other surfers.

Are you unmotivated and not really feeling like doing much of anything? None of us has to be heroes or break records. Keeping sharp mentally and staying in shape physically are perhaps the two most important things you must commit to. Eat healthy foods and challenge your mind in whatever way you choose, whether you put together a thousand-piece puzzle or create a garden. It is imperative that you be cognizant of all the essential ingredients for living your best life. It is ultimately your responsibility. Don't fall victim to laziness or lack of information. There are countless pieces of literature written on the subject of aging well, which includes nutrition, exercise, and lifestyle. Keeping yourself educated is a responsibility you must own.

Now, I know that not all of my suggestions were possible during the pandemic, but many are now viable. People of all ages are investigating areas of learning online. All it takes is a computer or smartphone and a willingness to keep improving yourself. Bridge and canasta are being played online, and countless classes are being offered in yoga, mindfulness, and meditation.

We were never a lackluster bunch and were hardly passive in the way we walked through the world. Starting a revolution did not allow for that. Don't throw in the towel now just because you lost a few important years. *Au contraire.* I urge you to make your plans and write them down. What is the first thing you will do now with your reprieve? And the next? And the one after that?

I guarantee that life will taste so much sweeter when you start living out your dreams.

III

Love

What About Love?

"Keep love in your heart. A life without it is like a sunless garden when the flowers are dead"
— Oscar Wilde

There is only one happiness in this life, to love and be loved"
— George Sand

Love is a canvas furnished by nature and embroidered by imagination"
— Voltaire

"Do not seek the because—in love there is no because, no reason, no explanation, no solutions"
— Anais Nin

Regardless of who is talking about love, one thing is for certain: We all need love in our lives. Love, however, can come in all shapes and forms. Unlike many other things in life, there is no right or wrong kind of love to receive or give if it's pure. It is said that love makes the world go round. Sadly, there has not been enough expression of love to sustain peace globally. But let us contemplate love on a more individual level. For most of us, finding romantic partners as we age is more precarious than when we were younger. We are not out in clubs, going to lots of parties, meeting people in class, or lingering at bars. By now, for some of us, our lives are spent a bit more at home, not necessarily sedentary but perhaps less social. If we are not married, then we are single, divorced, or widowed, and we might spend plenty of time by ourselves.

> *"Your task is not to seek for love, but merely to seek and find*
> *all the barriers within yourself that you have built against it"*
>
> — A Course in Miracles[43]

This is of particular importance to our generation because as we get older, we sometimes lose confidence and believe that love might be unobtainable. Let us take a second look at that notion. If you were lovable once, why do you feel you no longer are so? Is it because you have more wrinkles on your face? Is it because you have some physical challenges that you feel another person would not accept? Or is it that you have had too many broken relationships to feel like there is any hope of ever having success again in love?

I submit that you are not considering all your options. Oh, perhaps it is true that no one is sending you flowers or that you are not inundating the object of your desire with text messages. Maybe you are terrified to express how you feel about someone because you fear your love will not be returned. None of us is immune to being rebuffed, no matter how confident we might appear. As far back as when we were toddlers, we never liked to be told no or that we couldn't always get what we wanted. We're no longer teenagers or in our twenties, when we fell in love so easily and out of love perhaps just as fast. We trusted the feeling and went with it. As we grew older and experienced the pain of rejection, unfaithfulness, and the end of a love affair, perhaps we became more cautious or even distrustful of love. Where is it written that because we are now older, love should elude us?

As it relates to romantic love, what are your expectations? Do you feel you are past the age of enjoying that kind of relationship or even having access to it? Or do you feel that you have every right to experience it, hope to find it, and, most importantly, are open to it? The absence of a partner might be very disconcerting to you. You want to engage in life and have new experiences, but not alone. You crave affection, but it isn't there. You get into bed at night, and there is no one next to you to kiss good night or to snuggle and have great sex with.

---

43 Helen Schucman and William Thetford, eds., *A Course in Miracles: Combined Volume* (Course in Miracles Society, 2008), 338.

Beth

Beth's story is so sweet that I want you to enjoy it directly as she told it:

"At first, I felt self-conscious. At seventy-two, why did I suppose I was falling in love with a man I met at a dinner party with friends? Our backgrounds were vastly different, as were our ethnicities and social status, but we made this instant connection. He is very bright, and we talked all evening without even realizing that we were unintentionally ignoring the people around us. He asked for my number, but I didn't expect to hear from him. I don't know why, but I thought it might be a one-off. But he did call and ask me to dinner. Wow! I was so excited as I was getting ready to go on a date and greeting him at the door. It all felt unbelievable in a way. Honestly, I felt like a teenager. It was so crazy. But after a glass of wine, the jitters ceased, and I knew why we were both sitting there. There was a mutual recognition that this was something special. We have dated for just seven months, but it is clear that we are in love. Never, ever did I expect to be in this position again at this age. An additional bonus is that I feel so much younger, more vital, and, of course, happy.

"After living so long without love in my life and now having it, I've experienced an enormous reversal in how I move through life. I smile more at strangers, have more patience in general, and am more motivated to accomplish tasks. We decided to live together, and I don't know if that will lead to marriage. But for now, I am just soaking up the feeling, legally or not, and whatever happens from here is unknown. I love being in love."

"In your light, I learn how to love"

— Rumi[44]

---

44 Jalal al-Din Rumi, *The Essential Rumi*, trans. Coleman Barks, John Moyne (HarperOne, 2004), 122.

Table for One

Ask a friend who lost a partner how it feels to be alone. Most would say that it can feel quite lonely, especially when going out to parties and other events as a single. Eating meals alone has a different complexion than dining socially. Single people report eating dinner at the desk, on the sofa, in bed, or at the kitchen sink—and at a significantly faster pace. There are an estimated 38.5 million single-person households in America—approximately one-third of all total households, according to data collected in 2024 by the US Census Bureau.[45] As roughly one-third of baby boomers are single, many of these single-person households are occupied by older adults of our generation.[46]

There are times, however, when being alone provides room to be contemplative and make choices based solely on our own desires without having to get consent from a mate. We all know by now that nothing is perfect and everything has its pros and cons. Living on our own is another way of life that's no less significant than being partnered. For many, independence is the key to happiness. Myriad reasons contribute to a person wanting to be on their own. Perhaps you have been in relationships most of your life and would now like

---

45 United States Census Bureau, "Nearly Two-Thirds of U.S. Households Are Family Households," news release, November 12, 2024.
46 Bowling Green State University, "More Baby Boomers Facing Old Age Alone," *Science Daily*, April 16, 2012, https://www.sciencedaily.com/releases/2012/04/120416125154.htm.

to experience flying solo. Divorce in later life—or *gray divorce*, as it pertains to those over fifty—doubled between 1990 and 2010. As discussed earlier, roughly one in four divorces in 2010 occurred to persons aged fifty and older.[47] If that works for you, go for it. Single living can provide a host of new opportunities that were not available to you while you were in a relationship. Many activities are specifically designed to help single people engage with one another. Clubs and organizations bring single people together for a variety of reasons, not least of which is encountering your next companion, spouse, partner, travel buddy, friend, or whatever else you might be seeking.

The potential downside I see for boomers is that as we age, we confront many physical challenges. I believe it is perhaps better to have companionship so that if something unexpected were to occur, such as a fall or a stroke, there might be someone present to act immediately. Aside from health issues, as people grow older, there is often less social contact. Another detriment of living alone is isolation. Lack of interaction, as I have stated, has been proven to negatively affect health and longevity.

47 Susan L. Brown and I-Fen Lin, "The Gray Divorce Revolution: Rising Divorce Among Middle-Aged and Older Adults," *The Journals of Gerontology* 67, no. 6 (2012).

Love After Loss

Diana

Diana was a client before the pandemic, but our work together shifted dramatically as she focused on her loneliness. She is sixty-eight and has lived, for the most part, as an introvert. She was typically more comfortable at home by herself than in a group of people. Though Diana had lots of friends and acquaintances, she did not spend much time with them for a variety of reasons, not the least of which was that they all had busy lives.

Five months into the pandemic, she was reporting bouts of depression, anxiety, and sleeplessness. Intellectually, she understood that so many others were suffering the same manifestations, but emotionally, she felt frightened and in desperate need of companionship. The desperate part was most concerning, as I could not do anything to alleviate it. If Diana felt that way, I am certain many boomers experienced similar feelings and were craving the company of others. Reportedly, many boomers moved in with their children or at least moved geographically closer to them. But Diana did not have that option. She described it as feeling trapped, imprisoned, and hopeless. She wondered whether she would reach seventy and, if so, if she would still be living with masking and social distancing. What a terrible way to go out, she thought, and she regretted not taking advantage of more social opportunities in her senior years.

Life has a remarkable way of presenting opportunities when none seem to be obtainable. She received a call from an old college friend who was experiencing the same challenges and reached out just to make a connection. While they didn't live in the same state, they somehow decided that living together might assuage their loneliness and despair. It was Diana who decided to move because she felt she needed companionship so very much. She kept in touch with me by phone and sounded like a different person after she moved. She and her old friend were getting on very well together. She started volunteering at a florist near where they lived, and they did things together because they discovered that they had many common interests.

Diana had found a way to conquer her loneliness. An opening came along, and she walked bravely through and with certainty that this was the right thing for her in her senior years.

———————————◆◆———————————

"For beautiful eyes, look for the good in others; for beautiful lips, speak only words of kindness; and for poise, walk with the knowledge that you are never alone"
— Sam Levenson, from the poem "Time Tested Beauty Tips"[48]

We have often been dubbed the loneliest generation. What does it mean to be lonely? Simply living alone or in an isolated place might be just as harmful to your health as feeling lonely. Physical and

---

48 Sam Levenson, *In One Era & Out the Other* (Simon & Schuster, 1975).

mental health issues can put you at risk of loneliness and isolation, whether or not you are healthy. Meanwhile, those who are more socially connected live longer. A great deal of medical research has focused on the ramifications of loneliness. According to an article in AARP, when genomics researcher Steve Cole studied lonely men and women, he observed that "the blood cells appeared to be in a state of high alert, responding the way they would to a bacterial infection. It was as though the subjects were under mortal assault by a disease, the disease of loneliness."[49]

Social isolation has been defined as an objective measure that depends on the size of an individual's social network, while loneliness is more subjective, describing whether people feel they lack connections and companionship. A survey looked at the relationship between the loneliness of midlife and older adults and their connections to neighbors. Sixty-one percent of those surveyed who had never spoken to a neighbor felt lonely, compared with 33 percent of those who had spoken to a neighbor.[50] Connecting with our neighbors, I believe, has become very much a demographic issue, as there are parts of the country that tend to be more neighborly. It is also true that in urban areas, neighbors seem to be of less importance than they are in rural areas. Clearly, maintaining strong relationships with neighbors is instrumental in staving off loneliness and, in turn, living longer, healthier, happier lives.

Maddie

At sixty-eight, Maddie thought she was done with romance, and she came to me grieving that loss. She believed that part of her life was

---

49 Lynn Darling, "Is There a Medical Cure for Loneliness?" December 11, 2019, AARP website, https://www.aarp.org/home-family/friends-family/info-2019/medical-cure-for-loneliness.html.
50 Darcell Rockett, "Neighbors can impact your happiness, a study suggests. Chicago residents talk through their experiences," *Chicago Tribune*, October 21, 2019.

over, never to return. She thought she would never love again and never have that feeling of wanting someone badly. That notion caused her to be depressed and down on herself. She was washed up, too old for a fling, and did not believe she would ever again meet anyone to love.

And then the magic stepped in and started to do its thing.

It began with a fall. She slipped on some liquid in a supermarket and broke her hip. During her months of recovery, she hired a law firm to represent her in a lawsuit against the market.

A young attorney was assigned to her case, and Diana mostly had telephone meetings and updates with him. Finally, when she was well enough to go to the office for a meeting, she was told that her attorney had just left the firm and her case would be taken over by one of the senior partners. A bit dejected because she had spent many months talking with him about her case, she really did not want to go there again. Her dejection faded when an attractive older man walked into the office and greeted her with a warm apology. Suddenly, Diana was so grateful that the young attorney had made a timely disappearance.

You might guess where this is headed.

Once the case was settled—in her favor—she started dating her attorney. I'm so happy to say that they are now married. He had been widowed for a long time and wasn't in the dating scene. Still, he'd been hoping against hope that he would meet someone to spend the rest of his life with, and he did.

So, you see, there is always hope. You never know what is going to avail itself to you, so you must remain open to what comes your way. This story always makes me happy because I remember the first day Maddie came to see me, and I have witnessed the beautiful unfolding of her story.

––––––––––––– ◆◆ –––––––––––––

Of course, there are online dating websites where you can step out of your comfort zone and see what's out there. During COVID-19 confinement, we chose to FaceTime or Zoom with those we found interesting and possibly worth getting to know further. There is something very fascinating about meeting online and being forced to take time in becoming acquainted. This was a unique opportunity that the pandemic gave us. We were not able to rush into anything out of desperation and neediness.

You might be surprised to discover that your future love match awaits. But you must be willing to show up, be seen, and know you are deserving of love no matter your age, circumstances, health, or bank account. This is a fact of life. Give it a shot. What are you waiting for? Where is the downside?

Bennett

Bennett came to me in a terrible state after losing his wife of fifty years. He had married young, and at eighty, he had never known another woman. They'd shared children, grandchildren, and many happy memories. He felt like his life was over and thought it would have been a gift if he could have left with her. She had done everything for the household.

As money was no issue for him, I suggested that he hire someone to come in a few times a week to help him out with housekeeping, cooking, and laundry. At first, he was averse to the suggestion, but gradually, he agreed to give it a shot. His new housekeeper came to help him in more ways than he had anticipated. Also a boomer, she was a widow and understood the devastation and loneliness of losing a partner. She, however, had not had the longevity in her marriage that he'd had, as she was in her early sixties. But they talked a lot. After her work was done, they would sit and have kitchen table conversations about marriage, children, grandchildren, and life.

Bit by bit, he warmed to her and found himself thinking about her after she left at the end of the day. So he decided to employ her five days a week. Was there that much work to be done? Of course not. He was starting to consider her to be more than an employee and allowed himself to fantasize about asking her out for dinner. But he stopped himself because of the age difference, even though he knew that many couples have large age gaps. Still, he was terrified of rejection. Time passed, and they laughed and cried together. It was obvious they had found a connection, regardless of age or status. It became clear to both of them, so he went for it.

Today, they are living happily together and sharing families, and they're both so grateful that they found one another. Fear of rejection often keeps people apart. But really, when you think about it, what is the worst harm that can come from being rejected? I think it's just really a hurt ego. If you let that get in the way, you will miss many rich opportunities in life. Yes, you rely on your ego to guard your self-image, but how many times has it robbed you of positive relationships, work opportunities, and fulfilled dreams?

Rekindling the Spark

Please do not cower at this point in life. We are grown-ups, after all, and deserve all the benefits that were perhaps not socially acceptable in our younger years. The clock is ticking.

If you are partnered, now is a perfect time to revisit your initial attraction. If you have been together for a long time, look at your significant other and try to recall the early days, when you counted the minutes until you were together. Though time might have taken its toll in innumerable ways, is that person you look at each day the same basic soul you connected with originally?

The answer is highly subjective. A gentle reminder is needed, perhaps, to invest the time in really knowing who you both have become in your older years. Is the love still there? Perhaps it's not as impassioned, but is it solid and kind? Both of you have built a life together, perhaps had a family together, and have had decades of experiences together. You've created a loving montage of two people who made a commitment to share in the coalescing of your lives, for better or for worse. But perhaps you have had a change of heart.

I think it can be very meaningful to circle back to who you were as a couple when you were in your early years together and acknowledge the changes and the constants. When I was visiting my parents toward the end of their lives but before they both became ill, my mother was complaining about my father's memory and how he had a habit of repeating things he had just told her. His short-term memory was shot. My father had grown tired of my mother turning up the television very loud so she could hear it but refusing to acknowledge that she had a hearing deficit. They both were essentially having to accept each other at a time when aging kicks in with the attendant maladies.

I sat with both of them and asked my mother what it was about my father's poor short-term memory that upset her so much, other than it was exasperating at times. She burst into tears and told me it wasn't so much that it was so irritating to hear the same story repeatedly. The issue was that it was a sign of his getting older, and that frightened her.

My dad was just frustrated because he had been asking my mother to get hearing aids for a long while, and she had resisted. He felt she wasn't doing all she could to improve her situation.

They both knew what they needed to do.

While my dad probably couldn't do as much about his memory, she could try to accommodate her hearing loss. At that moment, when we were discussing their fears and anxieties at the kitchen table, I asked them both to stand up. They looked at me quizzically. Without music or any other accoutrements, I told my father to take my mother in his arms and dance and, while dancing, try to remember their teenage selves and how much fun they'd had throughout their lives together—especially as dance partners.

It was a spectacular breakthrough for both of them. They were able to let go of the frustrations they were each keeping inside and openly communicate about what was upsetting them. The strong love was there. That was obvious. But after over sixty years, they did not have the tools to express what they each needed. The short discussion and the dance created a moment I think I shall never forget. It was so very special.

The Skin We're In

Sex. Yes, I said sex because so many of us think those days are over. It has always amused me to hear younger people express surprise, and even shock, that their parents are still "doing it." Many older adults are enjoying sex. Approximately 73 percent of individuals aged fifty-seven to sixty-four, 53 percent of those aged sixty-five to seventy-four, and 26 percent of adults aged seventy-five to eighty-five say that they're sexually active.[51]

Think about it. There are no children around to rear, work life for many of us has terminated, and now we have time to play—golf, cards, bridge, and sex—whenever we feel so moved. Boomers have arrived at that sweet spot where there are no more constraints, and now it is time to indulge. According to Walter Bortz, geriatrics professor at Stanford Medical School, "If you stay interested, stay healthy and have a good mate, you can have good sex all your life. Best of all, it's good for you. There's strong data all over: It's a matter of survival." He says. "People that have sex live longer. People need physical connection. The more intimate the connection, the more powerful the effects."[52]

51 Penhollow TM. "Sexuality in Older Adults: Comprehensive Strategies for Clinicians and Patient-Centered Care," *American Journal of Lifestyle Medicine.* 2024;0(0). doi:10.1177/15598276241293100.
52 Jordan Heuvelmans, "Boomers are Having Lots of Sex and Loving It," February 14, 2020, Healthing website, https://www.healthing.ca/wellness/baby-boomers-are-breaking-sexual-taboos.

We have an open invitation to avail ourselves of a sensual smorgasbord, to sample from a bountiful buffet. So, why not take advantage of all the goodies? There are countless ads and commercials specifically designed for boomers who are looking to improve their sex lives. Other resources include videos demonstrating various aspects of lovemaking. While I don't think medications are necessarily the only answer, in some cases, they are necessary for sexual activity and in no way indicate an inadequacy of either party.

Orgasms contribute to well-being. Don't have a partner? What about a vibrator? You have innumerable buying options online, so there is no need to feel timid or embarrassed about walking into a store to make a purchase. Read the descriptions thoroughly and see which one fits your style. It is a worthwhile investment if you are looking for a sexual experience or perhaps prefer not to have one in the flesh. While vibrators are designed more for women, men have reported receiving pleasure from these sex toys as well. It depends on your predilections and physical areas of sensitivity.

Menopausal and postmenopausal women sometimes experience pain with intercourse, frequently due to vaginal dryness. As the vaginal wall becomes thinner and levels of estrogen are lower, there is less vaginal secretion. A water-based lubricant or lubricated condom can often lessen the pain. There are also medicated creams that can be effective. Men might struggle with erectile dysfunction, or ED, and medications are available to assist with that, providing there are no health constraints. This should not be seen as a failure but rather a medical function of aging. Blood circulation slows, blood pressure rises, and testosterone levels decrease. Testosterone and estrogen levels replenish overnight during the REM cycle and tend to be higher in the morning, increasing libido upon waking. Our bodies are primed for sex, with high levels of the hormone dopamine, which is at its peak after a night's sleep. Oxytocin (a.k.a. the love hormone), which is produced by the hypothalamus and released by the pituitary gland, is also at its highest upon waking, making you feel relaxed, happy, and ready to cuddle.

Research by Coventry and Oxford Universities indicates that more frequent sexual activity is linked to improved brain function, including verbal fluency.[53]   Sexual activity may even promote the growth of cells in the hippocampus, reducing memory loss. Sex burns about five calories per minute, according to Harvard Health Publishing.[54] That's about the same as going for a walk and qualifies as a light workout. But if you prefer the treadmill, it's up to you.

Enjoying an active sex life can be challenging at times, but there really are so many ways to work with what you have and still find lots of satisfaction. It's yours for the taking. A study conducted by *The New England Journal of Medicine* revealed that a bit more than a quarter of those aged seventy-five to eighty-five who participated claimed to have had sex in the past year, and more than half said they had sex at least two to three times a month. Almost one-quarter of those sexually active were having sex at least once a week.[55]

Cameron

Cameron was in great despair over the fact that he could not make love with intercourse. We spent time discussing what he felt was the obstacle to pleasing his partner. After much time together, we grieved over his inability to have an erection, but I managed to get through to him that there were many other ways to provide pleasure.

---

53 "More frequent sexual activity can boost brain power in older adults, according to new study," June 22, 2017, Coventry University website, https://www.coventry.ac.uk/primary-news/more-frequent-sexual-activity-can-boost-brain-power-in-older-adults-according-to-new-study-/#:~:text=study%20%7C%20Coventry%20University-,More%20frequent%20sexual%20activity%20can%20boost%20brain%20power,adults%2C%20according%20to%20new%20study&text=More%20frequent%20sexual%20activity%20has,universities%20of%20Coventry%20and%20Oxford.

54 "Is sex exercise? And is it hard on the heart?" August 25, 2022, Harvard Health Publishing, https://www.health.harvard.edu/healthbeat/is-sex-exercise-and-is-it-hard-on-the-heart#:~:text=Sex%20burns%20about%20five%20calories,be%20in%20shape%20for%20sex.

55 Stacy Tessler Lindau, MD, MAPP, Philip L. Schumm, MA, Edward O. Laumann, PhD, Wendy Levinson, MD, Colm A. O'Muircheartaigh, PhD, and Linda J. Waite, PhD, "A Study of Sexuality and Health among Older Adults in the United States," *The New England Journal of Medicine* 357 no. 8 (2007): 762-774. https://www.nejm.org/doi/full/10.1056/NEJMoa067423.

It took a while to convince him because he was fairly close-minded and felt terribly inadequate. It was all or nothing to him. I suggested he have an open discussion with his partner to see what she felt. He was surprised to learn she would be fine with making love, regardless of what they could not do, and focus on all the things that they could do together.

This is one of the greater success stories. Cameron, who was seventy-seven, gradually relaxed with his partner and started practicing new forms of lovemaking that had been unknown to him. He read books, watched films, and found that his interest in sexual possibilities was growing with great enthusiasm. It soon became evident that he had been stuck on basics and had not ventured out into the great libidinous unknown.

In time, something miraculous happened. What he'd thought had been permanently exiled from the kingdom came back with a vengeance, and his anxiety about not being able to penetrate his partner was yesterday's news.

Jim

Jim, age seventy-four, came to see me because he was massively depressed over his heart attack and believed he could no longer engage in sex. He was in heavy grief mode, so I was very careful with his feelings. As we delved deeper, I learned that he never exercised or went out socially and spent the majority of his time sitting on the couch, watching television. Upon further interrogation, I discovered that this was a self-imposed exile because he was terrified that he might incur another heart attack if he did anything physical. He did not suffer from ED or any other sex-related physical issues, but he had created his own obstacle based on neither fact nor medical admonition.

He received my directive: Go for a walk for ten minutes each day, gradually building to a half hour. Once he was comfortable with that, I suggested he go to a market and push a shopping cart around. At first, Jim didn't trust me and was reluctant to listen. But once I explained how much more dangerous it was to remain sedentary, he started to move. We slowly worked through his fears and reached the point where he was able to permit himself to engage in other activities again. The transformation seemed magical yet very perceptible.

Once the self-pity lightened up, Jim, like Cameron, educated himself by watching documentaries on healthy eating and exercising. He was already tech-savvy, so he joined user groups for men who have suffered heart attacks. Every day, he learned something from someone who had gone before him—some little jewel, a tip for this, a recipe for that. Ultimately, he dared to start practicing his golf swing at a local driving range, only to discover he had not lost his edge. Jim called a few of his golfing buddies, and he cautiously went from nine to eighteen holes in no time.

A new man was born.

His wife was obviously affected by his apprehension in the bedroom but waited patiently for him to come around. Fortunately, a hot topic among men in his user groups was sex after a coronary event, and it was mostly positive. No medical reason for abstinence could be documented. So, for the first time, he was getting the green light from peers—not a medical professional. While golf had its benefits, once he garnered his courage to have a sex life with his wife again, golf paled in comparison. His wife was thrilled with the change in him. And why not? They were both reveling in their unleashed passion and the pleasure that accompanied it.

◆◆

A large study published in *The American Journal of Cardiology* found that men who had sex at least twice a week were 50 percent less likely to die of heart disease compared with men who had it once a month.[56] In another study, British researchers followed 914 men for twenty years and found that as sexual activity increased, the risk of stroke and heart attack decreased.[57]

One Harvard study of almost 32,000 men found that the more a man ejaculated, the lower his risk of cancer. In fact, those who ejaculated more than twenty times per month reduced their prostate cancer risk by about 31 percent, compared with those who ejaculated four to seven times a month.[58]

Who knew?

A study published in *International Urogynecology Journal* found that sexually active women were significantly more likely to have a strong pelvic floor compared with those who were not sexually active. Every time you have sex, the muscles in your sex regions are getting a workout.[59] When you're aroused, muscle tension in the pelvic region naturally increases. During orgasm, all the muscles contract, just as they would during a Kegel exercise. Having strong pelvic floor muscles gives you control over your bladder and helps prevent incontinence. In men, a weak pelvic floor can contribute to erectile dysfunction. Another benefit to strengthening your pelvic floor is the potential to enhance your sexual experience. One study found that vaginal stimulation elevated pain tolerance by about 40 percent, while orgasm pushed it up nearly 75 percent.[60] During sex, endorphins—a naturally occurring pain reliever—are released, just as they are during other forms of physical exercise, such as running. When the body releases

---

56 Susan A. Hall, PhD, Rebecca Shackelton, MS, Raymond C. Rosen, PhD, Andre B. Araujo, PhD. "Sexual Activity, Erectile Dysfunction, and Incident Cardiovascular Events." *The American Journal of Cardiology* 105, no. 2 (2010): 192-197.

57 Shlomit Brandis Kepler, MHA, Tal Hasin, MD, Yael Benyamini, PhD, Uri Goldbourt, PhD, and Yariv Gerber, PhD. "Frequency of Sexual Activity and Long-Term Survival after Acute Myocardial Infarction." *Science Direct* 133 no. 1 (2020): 100-107.

58 "Ejaculation frequency and prostate cancer," January 19, 2022, Harvard Health Publishing, https://www.health.harvard.edu/mens-health/ejaculation_frequency_and_prostate_cancer.

59 Gregg Kanter, Rebecca G. Rogers, Rachel N. Pauls, Dorothy Dammerer-Doak, and Ranee Thakar. "A strong pelvic floor is associated with higher rates of sexual activity in women with pelvic floor disorders." *International Urogynecology Journal* May 21, 2015; 26 (7): 991–996.

60 Michelle Crouch, "12 Surprising Health Benefits of Sex After 50," November 17, 2022, AARP website, https://www.aarp.org/health/healthy-living/info-2022/surprising-sex-health-benefits-after-50.html#:~:text=Another%20study%20found%20that%20vaginal,the%20body's%20natural%20pain%20reliever.

hormones, such as oxytocin and prolactin, and neurotransmitters, a sense of calm prevails.

This topic is inescapable when talking about love or lack of it. Sex is a human need that does not necessarily have a biological clock. When I meet with married women and men who are grieving sexual relationships they once enjoyed with their spouses but no longer have, the craving surfaces. Single people long for it but have no partners, and some people in long-term marriages mostly seem disinterested in having sex with their partners. The thrill is gone.

Edward

I met Edward while on vacation in Europe. He and his wife were staying at the same hotel as I, and we found our paths crossing quite a bit. While we were having dinner separately in the hotel restaurant one evening, they invited me to join them. We soon found ourselves heavily engaged in topics ranging from politics to family. They were a charming older couple—sophisticated and highly educated. We talked about their careers and retired life. There was a perceptible air of tension but nothing spoken. Through conversation, they learned of my professional background, and the gentleman seemed especially interested.

When I was checking out of the hotel, the same gentleman noticed me and approached. "I wonder if we might talk again, as there is something I would like to discuss," he said.

I gave him my contact information and wished him well.

A few weeks later, I received an email from him, asking when we might talk. We got on a Zoom call, and it was then that he shared that he was sexually frustrated and longed for a sex life. His wife apparently had not been interested in years, and he was a faithful husband. What to do! We had a few more private sessions, but I told him that in order to have any hope of finding solutions, we had to bring his wife on board. At our next meeting, his lovely wife joined, already apprised of what had transpired. She acknowledged that her sex drive was long gone and thought he was foolish for still wanting to do what they did sixty-five years before

"Wait, hold on," I said. "Sixty-five years? Do you mind if I ask your ages?"

I'm ninety-one, and the wife is ninety," he replied.

Gulp, gulp. I was overjoyed. Overjoyed mostly because he personified what I already knew to be true: Desire does not have to die. It is so personal.

They shared that he was in reasonably good health and spirits, but she was less so. Maybe if she felt better. Maybe if she were younger. Maybe if she hadn't let herself go and maybe this and maybe that. Excuses. Lots of them. That's what we do as we get older. We feel less secure and play the age card. It's a convenient excuse.

We worked through much of their dissimilar feelings about sex, and they reached a truce. She would make herself available to him one night each week and not be dismissive of his advances. He had ingratiated himself with her by speaking candidly of his frustration and how sad and deprived of her he felt. .

As always, I followed up with them for the next month, and she had kept her word. He cherished her more than ever.

———————— ♦♦ ————————

Years ago, I did considerable research in the area of human sexuality, which involved interviewing hundreds of people, partnered and single. In an earlier book, I wrote about an elderly married couple who were living in an assisted living community but were not allowed to share a room. I was shocked and saddened that this couple, who were in their eighties and were holding hands when I interviewed them, revealed to me that they missed the warmth of sleeping together and the sex life they'd always enjoyed.

There can be many reasons why a person can no longer be capable of having an active sex life. For men, in particular, medications can have a direct effect on the ability to have an erection. But, as we all know, there are other ways to participate in an intimate relationship. Understandably, there is discernible desolation accompanying the fact that a man cannot engage in intercourse. Often, it feels emasculating, which is certainly reasonable. After all, men have been portrayed throughout the ages as the sexual conquerors—the stud gender. Again, the inability to have intercourse does not mean being sexually active is off the table. The whole body is a sensuous playground on which to play and have fun. It is worthwhile to explore all the different parts of your partner's body where you can create arousal and provide substantial satisfaction.

And don't forget for one moment who started the sexual revolution. It wasn't our parents from the fifties, who demanded that sex always be attached to marriage. We were the ones who liberated that notion. In turn, that led to very active, healthy sex lives back in the day—and to this day.

According to AARP, one in six adults over seventy are sexually active.[61] And why not? The boomers are perhaps the most sexually liberated demographic living today.

Although, with that comes the risk of potentially negative consequences. While women no longer have to worry about pregnancy, seniors seem to be reckless when it comes to using condoms and protecting themselves from STDs. According to statistics released by the American Medical Association, the number of cases of gonorrhea rose sixfold among Americans age sixty-five and older between 2010 and 2023, while cases of chlamydia cases more than tripled.[62] In 2018, syphilis was up 29 percent among people sixty-five and

---

61 Robin L. Flanigan, "The Secrets of Sex Over 40: 8 Questions Answered," September 29, 2023, AARP website, https://www.aarp.org/home-family/friends-family/info-2023/sex-over-40-study.html.
62 Jennifer Lubell, "With STIs on rise among older adults, here's what doctors can do," January 6, 2025, American Medical Association website, https://www.ama-assn.org/delivering-care/population-care/stis-rise-among-older-adults-here-s-what-doctors-can-do#:~:text=Rates%20of%20syphilis%2C%20gonorrhea%2C%20and,Fryhofer%20explained.

older.[63] Practicing safe sex should be a priority for all sexually active individuals, regardless of age. Untreated chlamydia and gonorrhea in women can lead to pelvic inflammatory disease, which may lead to chronic pelvic pain.[64] Men with untreated chlamydia can also experience painful infections and swollen joints.

Vanessa

Vanessa was a frequent participant in the early free love movement and had quite a few sexual encounters. Her desire for sex did not wane as she got older, and she continued to enjoy many sexual experiences. Marriage was not her thing, so she dated and had some long-term relationships, but nothing stuck. She considered herself rather savvy when it came to sex and brought that along with her as she became an older woman. She continued to take pleasure in the opposite sex and was unapologetic.

At first, I was surprised that she came to me as a client, as our initial conversation did not reveal any major conflicts or problems. Shortly after, however, she exploded. She was diagnosed with human papillomavirus, or HPV, and it had a rather strong impact on her. She had developed vaginal lesions, and her doctor told her they were precancerous. While this was hardly a death sentence, it really shook her up.

$$\cdot \bullet \bullet \cdot$$

63 Brian P. Dunleavy, "What Is Syphilis? Symptoms, Causes, Diagnosis, Treatment, and Prevention," updated December 21, 2022, Everyday Health website, https://www.everydayhealth.com/syphilis/guide/.

64 "How long can a person have chlamydia before it causes damage?" the Medical News Today website, https://www.medicalnewstoday.com/articles/what-happens-if-chlamydia-is-untreated.

Boomers need to get with the program and understand that just because we can't get pregnant now, we are not protected from venereal disease unless we take precautions. Women, as well as men, need to have a supply of condoms on hand so that perilous fluids are not exchanged and they can continue to enjoy sex for the rest of their days.

What did we shout? "Make love, not war"?

Vanessa had managed to ride the wave of the sexual revolution unscathed by disease. But time and negligence had caught up with her. It was a learning experience, to be sure, but one that left her highly reticent about engaging in sex again. She needed a good amount of counseling to calm her nerves and fully understand that what she'd contracted was most likely not going to go anywhere and that, with treatment, she would be fine. But there are no guarantees. So, if you are dating but not in a long-term relationship, I strongly suggest that you take all precautions and do some reading and your own research so you don't go into it blindly.

Be smart about sex. While we are not the hookup generation, we actually might still have the mindset of the sixties, during which we were open to sex in all its glory. The onus should not be on the man alone. Is this not the time to bring levity to our lives? We have done all the hard work. Now it's time to sit back, or lie down, and have a lot of laughs and gratification.

In the seventies, while attending UCLA, I conducted extensive research in the field of human sexuality. My thesis was titled "The Evolution of the Vibrator and Its Impact on Female Sexuality." How well I recall my counselor being in shock when I handed in my proposal and reminding me that this was UCLA, not Berkeley!

For those of you unfamiliar with the University of California school system, Berkeley has always been the more liberal of the bunch, albeit an outstanding academic institution. At the time, UCLA was a bit more conservative. But sex is sex. It never goes out of style or asks for your academic credentials or political persuasions. Actually, she was in disbelief when I immediately found a thesis advisor at the Neuropsychiatric Institute on campus and the board approved my topic!

Women who heard of my study on vibrator usage as a tool for sexual enhancement contacted me, begging to be interviewed. All of them wanted to sing of their freedom. They also wanted to learn more about what was accessible, what was acceptable, and how they could actualize emancipation from the "good girl" sensibility of the fifties. So, who were all these women longing to thrive on an equal playing field as their male counterparts? They were you. They were me. They were the boomers then and the boomers now. So, proceed with the same bravado and know that there are still lots of treats waiting for you to taste.

Tony

Sometimes, when I see clients who are grieving over a particular loss, another loss that lay dormant for years will unravel while we're working together. It is fascinating.

Tony was grieving the loss of his wife of twenty-five years when he came to see me. She had passed away two years earlier, but in our process, he revealed that he could not bring himself to date. We talked about how he might have feelings of guilt, even though his wife was gone and would have wanted him to live his life. But as we dug deeper, he revealed that he was terrified of having to perform sexually. His sex life with his wife had not been very fulfilling, and he felt he had lost his ability to approach a woman, knowing it would eventually lead to the bedroom. It seems his wife had been hypercritical of his lovemaking techniques and rejected his advances most of the time. He'd developed unrealistic insecurities, but they were seemingly justified. She had been very sexually active when she was single, experimented extensively with sex, and dated some high-powered men. Tony felt intimidated by her past. It manifested in feelings of inadequacy.

Our work together was a mix of grief recovery and sex counseling, and we reached a point where he felt confident enough to get out of his shell and investigate the dating scene. As a second-stage boomer in his early sixties, he did not face the age discrimination that the early boomers faced. He signed onto dating sites, joined a singles hiking club, and eventually went on a singles cruise. He could not remain in the background any longer.

He started to enjoy himself again and found new meaning in his life and pursuits. One day, I opened the mail to find an envelope filled with photos of Tony and a woman, laughing, hugging, kissing, and smiling. Hoping this wasn't a rebound situation, I was thrilled, nonetheless, to see him looking so happy. The next time we met, I received all the details of his chance meeting with someone in his hiking group. She had just joined, and the sparks flew. It is too soon at this writing to know if the relationship will last, but the point is that he regained his confidence and was back in the game

Emma

Emma was miserable and more than a little desperate, hopeless, and dejected. It came as no surprise that she made the effort to reach out to me, but she doubted very much whether there was any solution for her. There is always a challenge in working with grievers, as breakthroughs do not necessarily come easily. But therein lies the challenge. Slumped in her chair and appearing fed up, she blurted out her despair. No guesswork was required on my part. Emma needed assistance, and it became clear that she chose to see me not just because I am a grief and loss coach but because I have worked extensively in the field of human sexuality.

Emma was sixty-eight years old and had not been able to have sex since she was fifty-nine because it meant she would incur a lot of pain and difficulty. She had reached menopause early and couldn't take hormones because she had a history of breast cancer. She lacked the secretion that would naturally provide more comfort and allow her to have intercourse. She confided that a friend suggested Vaseline, which Emma said did nothing. Her gynecologist told her to begin inserting tampons, starting with the smallest size and gradually going to the largest size, to see if she could stretch her vaginal opening. It was a big fail. Emma had vital years ahead for engaging in sexual activity, but she wanted to be able to have intercourse, not just the foreplay.

To be candid, I had a lot of empathy for her but no guarantees to offer. Her dilemma affects countless women who are at the age of gradually losing estrogen and not being able to replace it with hormones. The best I could offer was to reiterate what she most likely already knew: There are always new treatments on the market, and the idea is to stay current and keep trying. While one product might not work, the new flavor of the month might just do it. Unfortunately, I could share with her only what is already known about her diagnosis.

Even if you're menopausal or postmenopausal, you don't have to deal with painful sex. Treatment helps with symptoms and restores a healthy pH and bacterial balance in your vagina. Don't avoid sexual activity if you have vaginal atrophy. A lack of sexual activity actually worsens the condition. Sex stimulates blood flow in the vagina and aids in the production of fluids. Therefore, sex actually keeps the vagina healthy.

Emma felt a little bit more optimistic at the end of our session. Knowing that many women experience her condition, she was going to take one of my suggestions and start searching online for a support group for women to see what she might cull from others. She promised to be more proactive and relentless in her search for solutions. Naturally, I reminded her of all the many possibilities in ways to engage during sex without actual penetration. Her spirits were higher, and I let her know I would be communicating with her to follow up on her progress. She simply had to address her sexual health.

—————————◆◆—————————

A large body of research has found that sexual activity and intimacy are linked to lower rates of depression, stress, anxiety, and feelings of isolation. Plus, regular sexual activity can boost happiness and mood. One of the more recent studies published in *The Journal of Sexual Medicine* found that anxiety and depression scores were significantly lower in those who were sexually active during the COVID-19 lockdown compared with those who weren't.[65] Stress was so prevalent in our households while we all wondered whether the pandemic was to be the new normal or just a passing trend.

The stress was channeled in very distinct ways. We ate too much, we imbibed too much, and, oh, the innumerable movies we streamed. Did you become an avid reader or bake just a touch too often? So many of us just became lazy, self-indulgent slugs, while others focused on fear and anxiety. But either way, we were less physically active in quarantine. No hiking or running or power walking for us. Rather, we walked frequently back and forth to the refrigerator. But had we focused more on sex, we might have avoided those COVID-19 extra pounds.

Of course, how many calories you actually burn depends on how long your session lasts and how vigorous it is. But even if your romp lasts only six minutes—the typical length of a session—that's still better than doing nothing at all. The latest research on physical activity reveals that getting your heart rate up even for just a few minutes has health benefits.

If you're not convinced, how about the people who live in Ikaria, Greece? It's one of the regions of the world where people live significantly longer than average. More than 80 percent of people ages sixty-five to one hundred there are having sex, according to Blue

---

65 Daniele Mollaioli, Andrea Sansone, Giacomo Ciocca, Erika Limoncin, Elena Colonnello, Giorgio Di Lorenzo, and Emmanuele A. Jannini, "Benefits of Sexual Activity on Psychological, Relational, and Sexual Health During the Covid-19 Breakout," *The Journal of Sexual Medicine* 2020 Oct 23;18(1):35–49.

Zones, an organization that researches the world's longest-living cultures.[66]

And yes, as quiet as it is kept, there is a divide between men and women. They function differently in sex. Women typically want an emotional connection with their partners. But too often in long-term partnerships, sex is performed by rote. It becomes a quickie without foreplay, which women very much need—just as they need an orgasm.

---

66 Aislinn Kotifani, "The Link Between Good Sex, Good Health, and Longevity," Blue Zones website, https://www.bluezones.com/2020/05/the-link-between-good-sex-good-health-and-longevity/.

Love Comes in All Shapes and Sizes

Maybe you are not looking for romance, and that's perfectly okay. If you are a leading-edge boomer, maybe you enjoyed enough romantic relationships in the past and are quite content without one now. So, we need to explore where you might find love in other places.

Well, I contend that if you are fortunate enough to have grandchildren, you must recognize by now that there is an abundance of love to be had with them. This is a hot topic for me. Many people say they enjoy their grandchildren more than they did their children because they can spoil grandkids. Then, when grandparents have had their fill, they can return the children to their rightful owners. I admit I love being a mom first, so I do not subscribe to that. However, I savor every moment I have with my grandchildren. They are boundless love and fill my heart with so much warmth and pleasure.

Think about that for a moment. If you want love in your life and are a grandparent, there is nothing like the feeling of a child running into your arms, sitting on your lap for story time, or baking chocolate chip cookies with you. Believe me, I do get it when people say they prefer being grandparents to being young parents. Now we have the time and the wisdom to shower our children's children with endless love. If we're lucky, we get it back tenfold. This is a time when we can do some of the things we were too pushed to do when we were rearing our own little ones. We are on the periphery of our grandchildren's lives, so we are more apt to get the hugs and kisses and little of the bickering.

Maybe you are not an actual grandparent by blood, but you might be a stepmother, godfather, aunt, or uncle to a child. The same thing applies. You can carve out a very special relationship with that child and have it be meaningful and loving. And, by the way, age does not matter. Grown grandchildren can feed you with love, and you can reciprocate in kind. The point here is that there is much love to be enjoyed if only you take advantage of it. Sometimes, we are reticent to reach out to young adults because we assume they would rather spend their free time with their friends. While that might be true, just as in any relationship, you need to ask for what you want. Suggest getting together for lunch, a movie, or whatever mutual interests you might share. I went to all my grandson's basketball games, and I know he was happy that I was in the stands to cheer him on. He always thanked me for being there, and I was so filled with pride while watching him on the court. He also finishes every phone call with "I love you so much," as do my granddaughters, with variations on the theme.

Most schools have a Grandparents' Day, which is a lovely time to visit your grandchild's school and see what they do there. In elementary school, children typically put on plays and concerts, which you can attend with great satisfaction as you watch your little one perform.

However, I understand that we don't all live near our grandchildren, as families have spread out so much. Some grandparents get to see children only on holidays or during visits. Speak with your child and learn when your grandchild might be having a recital or a performance of some kind that you could attend. If your grandchild goes away to summer camp, that's another excellent time to visit and see them in that environment. I still have memories of visiting days at summer camp and seeing all my grandparents there with my parents. I felt very lucky because some campers had none.

No children in your purview? You know what is coming next. Have you considered a kitty or a puppy, perhaps? It's wonderful to be providing a home for an animal while also having a loving companion for yourself.

You can see the amount of good animals provide in hospitals, for example, where pets are brought in to brighten a patient's day. Tactile stimulation that comes with having an animal makes another good case for having a pet for a pal in your older years. This is so vital because, as we age, we are typically not touched enough—and being touched is a critical component of feeling loved and enjoying general well-being. You can cuddle and snuggle with a pet without much fear of rejection. I have never known a cat to beg not to be stroked or a cuddly dog to reject affection.

But be realistic with size and upkeep as to what you can manage comfortably, both physically and financially. Pets can cost untold amounts of money if they get sick or have chronic physical problems. It is important to understand your circumstances and limitations. Do you live in an area where it is easy to go out for a walk with your dog? Do you travel a lot and would have to board your dog? Would you be comfortable with that? Are you still working and would need to hire a dog walker during the day? That would mean giving someone else entrée to your home. There are also grooming and food costs. For cats, you would also need a litter box, litter, and maybe a scratching post.

My intention is certainly not to dissuade you, because I think having a pet is absolutely the best thing in the world, even if you are partnered. It is just important to weigh all the responsibilities before deciding to adopt a sweet, furry creature.

You can choose your friends. But how many of you have wonderful families and equally wonderful relationships with family members? For those of you who do, count yourself among the fortunate ones. A fun, intact family was all I knew until I became an adult and discovered that many families are not quite like that. As a child, I took life for granted and just assumed that everyone grew up in a beautiful home and had a home-cooked meal every night, nice, clean clothes to wear to school, bedtime stories, summer camp, beach club memberships, and even college. I thought that just came with the territory. It would be wonderful to have a second chance to thank my parents for all they gave me.

Think about your family. Many of us are in senior positions in our families now, with children and grandchildren following our lead.

There is boundless love to receive from family members on so many different levels. I am madly in love with my grandchildren. Hugs and kisses go a long way when the little ones sit on your lap or snuggle with you for a sleepover. During the quarantine days of the pandemic, I was so saddened by the inability to enjoy the physical tenderness we shared. Like so many of us, we Zoomed, joked, wondered, and asked questions for which we had no answers—mostly, "When will this end?"

What about siblings? If you have one, is your relationship loving? Do you feel you could depend on them if you were in need? What about fun? Do you have family members with whom you engage in fun activities? Try to reach out if you can. Distance often makes it impossible to be with extended family. But sometimes, we make too little effort to insert ourselves into familial relationships. Many people are looking for family through genealogy and have discovered relations unknown to them living in the same city. New family connections might prove to be very loving.

My family means everything to me. But you might feel differently, and that's okay.

Deep and significant friendships can be vessels of intense and lasting love. True friends provide comfort, support, and love that can last a lifetime. Unlike with blood relatives, we can choose to seek out those with whom we share common interests and a meaningful history. There are infinite experiences to be enjoyed with friends, and over time, there are expressions of love that cannot be denied.

Love comes in many different guises, and it is important to recognize a loving gesture as it presents itself so you can receive it in the way that it is meant for you,

Cooking is a hobby I have enjoyed most of my life. Cooking from scratch, the way I prefer, is labor-intensive. First, there is the hunt for all the perfect ingredients. Then the food must be washed, sliced, or diced. From there, it is time to bake, broil, grill, stir fry, or air fry. As I proceed, I generally wash the pots and pans as I use them so that the kitchen is uncluttered and there won't be a pile-up waiting for me at the end. This isn't a cookbook. So, why am I expounding about the joys of cooking? I love having dinner parties for a small group of friends and cooking family dinners for all the holidays. Many friends have told me I should open a restaurant, and my response is always the same: Though I enjoy it, cooking, for me, is a labor of love. Sitting down with friends and family and spending an evening over a meal is about love. We taste and talk, and it becomes a loving event. I know I have provided something that will be enjoyed.

A stretch? None at all. Just another avenue for giving and receiving love.

Paige

Paige, a divorcee in her late sixties, was working with me on the sudden loss of her son. She was overwhelmed and disoriented. Of course, she was devastated and in shock. She had no siblings, but she did have a lifelong best friend. Her friend jumped in and had her back in every possible way. She made all the funeral arrangements, slept at Paige's house so she would not be alone, made phone calls to spread the tragic news, and ordered food for the repast following the service, always holding Paige's hand.

Is this not love? Can it be defined in any other way?

When we give from the heart, it is a selfless expression of love, whether it is going on a shopping trip because your friend wants your input or giving up plans you have made because your friend is suffering and needs you. A friend sometimes offers more loving support than a partner does and often has more energy to give to the task. Just as love, by definition, is unconditional, so is true friendship.

Self-Love

"To love oneself is the beginning of a life-long romance"
— Oscar Wilde
"If you have the ability to love, love yourself first"
— Charles Bukowski
"Self-love, my liege, is not so vile a sin, as self-neglecting"
— William Shakespeare

Here we move on to what is, for most of us, the most challenging form of love—self-love. Before you can love another, you must first love yourself. Those words have been spoken so often as to become cliché. It sounds rather simplistic. You might be thinking, Of course I love myself. I think I'm a great person who treats others well. I respect nature and am kind to animals. I volunteer when called upon and donate to charities. So yes, I love myself. I am a good person. Does that define a person who necessarily loves herself? Not really. That describes a person who does good deeds and cares for others. But what I'm talking about here is loving oneself the way we give love to others.

If you ever had a friend who called you to say she needed you because she felt alone or a family member who reached out because he was in despair, I am guessing you were there for that person out of love. So here is the question: Who do you turn to when you are in need of love? Your partner? Your friend? Your mother? Your daughter?

So therein lies a potential proposition. What if you are out of options and everywhere you turn is temporarily out of order? But you really, really need love, and you need it now. According to Gautama Buddha, you yourself, as much as anybody in the entire universe, deserve your love and affection. How does that strike you? Does it sound selfish? Self-serving? Narcissistic maybe?

All of these notions could not be further from the truth.

Charlie

Here are Charlie's words about this topic:

"I have worked hard my whole life, rarely taking time to smell the flowers. My main concern was providing for my family. Once retired, I found that I had many projects to complete around the house that had been overlooked for years. It was overwhelming at first, but then I learned to break it down to one project at a time with no hard and fast deadline. I soon came to the realization that I never took time out for myself. After retirement, I was continuing to provide for my family, just in a different way. It was obvious that I was still not putting myself on top and doing anything expressly for me.

"Always a good athlete, I had not made time for sports in decades. Some of my buddies played pickleball, racquetball, and tennis. It was very difficult for me to take the first step, but I decided to start playing tennis again and joined my friends for a weekly game. Not only was I getting much-needed exercise, but I was interacting with others and taking that time just for me each week. I developed a heightened sense of importance in a way that punctuated that I mattered too. It felt so good. And best of all, my wife was thrilled to see me become interested in something outside the home."

Charlie discovered that by making himself a priority once a week, he felt freer from daily obligations. It did not make him selfish or greedy. He understood that he mattered and deserved the benefits that his long years of caring for others brought him. He was caring for Charlie. He was showing himself love by carving out time to enjoy a sport and the camaraderie that went with it. The emphasis had shifted to himself, yet not to the exclusion of those he loved. In that process, he recognized that guy he'd known fifty years prior.

———————◆◆———————

Some of us are very good at self-care, while others are not. But self-care is integral to loving ourselves. When you wake each morning and think about how you will spend your day or make a to-do list, where do you rank in the prioritizing of what is essential?

Once again, I must reference the pandemic and how it impacted our lives. We were at home much more than we ever had been. For some, that meant more free time to indulge. For others, it might just have felt frustrating because they were used to going out and conducting their daily lives at the office or pursuing other interests. Being quarantined inside forced us to be with ourselves. How did that play out for you? The voice in your head dictates how you feel about yourself. Ultimately, that—not how others perceive you—is all that really matters.

So go for it. Love yourself with all your heart, spirit, passion, and soul. Maybe you need to check in with your feelings of self-worth. To love yourself, you have to feel deserving of love. It seems so obvious, doesn't it, that, of course, we love ourselves. But it really is not that simple. We go through the motions of life, being good human beings for the most part. But do we really practice self-love?

Do you feel worthy of love? When you make a mistake, do you say to yourself, "Oh, what a loser I am"? I know that each of us has spent time criticizing ourselves for mistakes we made. And yet, would you be that critical of your best friend? Or would you more likely suggest that she stop beating herself up? You must treat yourself the way you treat others—a kind of twist on "Do unto others as you would have them do unto you."

Do unto you, and be less critical, less self-deprecating, and more compassionate.

Jaqueline

Jaqueline tells her story in heartbreaking but inspiring words:

"After losing my husband, I had to learn how to love again. I did not have any family to lavish love upon, nor was I interested in dating. I missed loving someone the way I'd loved Jesse. A friend suggested I speak with a coach, which I disregarded for a while as unnecessary. Then, out of desperation and up against the defeatist wall, I started counseling. My coach was very compassionate and listened to me for weeks.

"One day, she asked me a question I was unprepared for: 'Can you love yourself?'

"I wasn't at all sure how to respond or even how to implement loving myself. The very notion seemed vague and unrealistic. I started reading books and listening to podcasts that taught the philosophy of self-love. Wow, what an eye-opener that was for me. Happily and voluntarily, I had given all my love to my partner and never once stopped to consider myself along the way. On its face, it sounded selfish to think about expending loving energy on me. But as I uncovered layers in my coaching sessions, I saw a new reality—one that allowed for and promoted the idea of doing nice and loving things for myself.

"But that was not enough. There was much more to it than that. Loving me was another hurdle. It was a totally new concept, but it was one I knew I had to adopt and welcome into my life. It did not come easily or quickly. But it did come in time, and I am happier now than I have ever been. I feel so good about myself in a way I never imagined or even thought possible."

◆◆

*"I don't trust people who don't love themselves and tell me
'I love you'"*

— Maya Angelou[67]

For some people, loving themselves appears to be part of their DNA, but I would suggest that we are not born with self-love. We can be self-centered, perhaps. But self-love is sometimes learned at an early age from a role model, parent, or older sibling. For most, it does not come naturally. Some people appear to be extremely confident and give the impression of loving themselves to a great degree. In truth, many who seem to function at maximum capacity and be very happy with their lives and all their accomplishments do not necessarily love themselves. They might love the self-image they have created but do not authentically love themselves with the same commitment they so freely extend to others.

Why wouldn't we love ourselves? We have come this far in our lives, and we know there are some things about ourselves that we still might not understand and perhaps are not even interested in understanding. But what would stop us from loving ourselves?

Perhaps it started in childhood, when certain insecurities left indelible marks or when you found yourself ridiculed by a critical parent or teacher. Subconsciously, you fought back. You wanted to prove your worth and do everything perfectly, but then you became like Sisyphus and never quite got to the top of your game. Maybe you became a high achiever with all the obvious accolades. But when you go to bed each night, are you consciously grateful to yourself? Do you bless and tell yourself how much you love yourself?

We have all been guilty of negative self-talk, but be aware of it and move outside yourself when doing it. Treat yourself as kindly as you would a friend. Acknowledge that what you are feeling and thinking is not helpful and is often harmful to your spiritual, mental, and physical health.

Please do not confuse this with narcissism. There is a delicate balance between putting yourself at the center of the universe and

---

67 Maya Angelou, "Spelman College Commencement Speech," 1992, posted May 28, 2014, by Spelman College, YouTube, https://www.youtube.com/watch?v=70RH-h7QfP0.

showing gratitude and love in your own very personal universe. A narcissistic person has an inflated sense of self-importance, a need to be admired, and a total lack of empathy. Most likely, that is not you.

What I am speaking to is the ability to listen to yourself with compassion, nurture yourself when you are feeling needy, embrace yourself when you seek support, and commend yourself on your achievements, no matter how small.

Be your own best friend.

"You, yourself, as much as anybody in the entire universe, deserve your love and affection"

— Buddha

Reflection

"The future belongs to those who believe in the beauty of their dreams"
— Eleanor Roosevelt

Think about the time spent on your regrets—hours ruminating over poor decisions and fantasizing about do-overs, the lifestyle you thought you would have in your senior years blunted by the cold snap of life. By now, you must recognize that none of us is perfect. But as your cheerleader, I urge you to embrace the glaring truth that you are a boomer—a lifetime member of a generation of renegades, activists, forward thinkers, music makers, innovators, peace seekers, and spiritual practitioners. Wear it like a gold medal. No matter where you have been and what life lessons you have learned, you have lived through a time so rich that even the most prescient of us could not have imagined it. So, in loving yourself, you are loving all that has made you into the whole person you are at this moment. That is enough because this is who you are now.

Moving forward, there will always be challenges. My goal is not to offer a panacea for all things boomer. My intention is to revisit some of our past and some of our present, then offer ideas and thoughts to consider for our future. When pondering what is next, you can affect only what is in your control. But in doing so, it is incumbent upon you to remember that regardless of what situation you find yourself in, there is always hope. It's so cliché, but it's a notion I urge you to adopt as your own. We all hope that, regardless of the pandemic that sapped us and instilled fear in our very beings, we are resuming our lives as fully as we choose to, though it might not be the lives we left behind. Again, this is a beautiful opportunity. Think of this time as nascent and promising. Approach it with the same appetite and urgency that you had when you broke ground as a boomer.

By now, you have learned that your focus does not have to be on all the social trappings that might have caught your attention in your younger years. You want to enjoy yourself, have inner peace, know that your family is thriving, maintain good health, have a few good friends, and hope that you have made a difference, no matter how minor and seemingly insignificant.

While writing these words, I received a phone call from someone I knew long ago. He was able to locate me through social media. We talked for a while and spoke of our first encounter. Because we had a friendship then, I was happy to hear from him thirty years later. But most of all, what he revealed to me on that call sincerely touched me. He told me I had made a big impact on his life at a time when he was struggling emotionally and needed someone with whom he could exchange thoughts and feelings. He'd needed to be heard. He went into detail about how he found me to be so genuine amidst a sea of people who were not. He knew that when I asked him how he was doing, I meant it. When we met, he was a college freshman struggling with family issues and working part-time. I always tried my best to be available and listen. He is now a happily married man with two beautiful daughters, and I was so warmed by the words he shared with me. Isn't that what it's about, after all?

If we have learned nothing else from the pandemic, we must acknowledge that reaching out to each other is so important. I didn't know his politics, and he didn't know mine simply because it just didn't matter. We were just two human beings, years and worlds apart, who had made a connection. Apparently, I gave him something he needed at the time, which helped him get through. When we judge people because of how they look or their age or their social standing, we are doing ourselves a disservice because we never know what lies behind a person's veneer. Many life lessons have come to me through those with street smarts rather than college educations.

Frosting

Frosting can be a substance that covers the ground
The layer of pink that dresses a cake
Or a romance newly found
The rays of the sun on a placid lake
A merchants' display at Christmas time
Or a high fashion model walking to rhyme
The outer part of man is skin
This is the frosting to which he's akin
But the inner part known as the soul
Too often portrays him in a different role
He can be covered with happiness that looks so true
While beneath it all lies a heart so blue
He is merry and joyful to all can see
But sad and forlorn in reality
So recognize in man his character and deed
Be selective, choose wisely and then take heed.

— Susan Dean, age 13

My life has been exponentially enriched by taking time to talk with and sometimes form lasting friendships with people of all professions and backgrounds. I discovered that my long-time trash collector was a single dad bringing up three children, all of whom he put through college. He loved theater, flew to New York periodically to see Broadway shows, and traveled to Europe to ski. He worked hard, got paid well, and managed his life in the best possible way for him. I am certain that to most of my neighbors, he was just the man who hauled away our trash. I am guessing they were mostly dismissive of him, but he was so much more than his job. He was a man who cared about family, culture, and sports. He didn't have the opportunity to attend college, so he found work that would bring in substantial hourly pay and afford him the lifestyle he enjoyed and the ability to give his three children a good quality of life.

"A simple smile. That's the start of opening your heart and being compassionate to others"

— Attributed to Dalai Lama

For twenty years, I privately looked after a homeless man who panhandled under a freeway overpass. I passed him every morning en route to my office. At this particular corner, there was a very long traffic light. So I had the opportunity to say a few words to him—mostly "Good morning" and "I hope you have a nice day today." I told him I would not give him money but would be happy to give him food and a smile. Our conversation progressed from exchanging perfunctory salutations to health and needs. He asked nothing of me. He, like so many others, had lost his fortune and family to drugs and now was living on the street. Did that make him a bad person in my eyes? No, he'd made mistakes. But who of us hasn't?

One day, he questioned why I cared about him and took the time to bother with him. I simply told him, "We both bleed the same. We both care about our children. But I have a roof over my head, and you do not." My upbringing taught me to value and care about all human beings, especially those less fortunate. He prevailed upon me to allow him to repay me in any way he could. Upon learning that he used to work for a landscaper and could do any kind of gardening, I immediately told him I was facing my annual brush clearance inspection, and there were many hours of yard work to be done.

The deal was sealed. Every Sunday morning, I met him at the bus stop and brought him to my home, where he raked and piled and sweated and exhausted himself, at which point he would lie down on a lounge chair next to the pool and take a late-afternoon nap.

Eventually, he joined my family and me for Sunday dinners. Admittedly, it was more than a little risky, but it worked.[68] He became part of our family, participating in topical conversations and showing a lot of interest in my young children. Many years later, he told me I gave him something worth so much more than the dollar bills and food he collected on the street—a feeling of humanity.

---

68 I would never do that today. Somehow, the world felt kinder then. But in the decades to follow, we've learned that we cannot open our doors to strangers at all. Please don't judge.

We never know how our words or actions might influence another person, either positively or negatively. It takes very little effort to show that you care about someone. But that effort can be life-changing for the recipient and especially for the giver.

"The more we care for the happiness of others, the greater is our own sense of well-being"

— Dalai Lama XIV[69]

So, to all of you boomers out there, I encourage you to keep on rocking and feeling *groovy* every day. We deserve respect as representatives of the senior community, and I urge you to be vocal when you encounter ageism. An Age Wave report states, "We're witnessing the beginning of a complete paradigm shift as today's modern elders dismantle the long-held cultural beliefs and social norms about how older women and men should think, feel, and act. At the same time, the older adult population is about to skyrocket by more than 50% over the next 30 years. Today's modern elders are eager to pursue new dreams, adventures, and goals as they enter a whole new chapter in life."[70]

From Mae West's lips: "You're never too old to become younger."[71]

It is very convenient to dismiss us as a generation that has aged out of the important conversations because we seemingly have little to speak to. We have said our piece, and now we are closer to deterioration without much to bring to the party, as if we'd be invited. That does not describe you or me. *Deterioration?* How about *excitation* instead?

Perhaps it is true that some of our joints need oiling or even replacing, but that in no way should depreciate our greatness. Pity those young ones who declare themselves too omnipotent to acknowledge the boomers who have gone before them—we who have carved the ultimate model for change. I am endlessly amused when I'm buying an appliance or an electronic device and a salesperson young enough to be my grandchild tells me that I can buy a twenty-year extended warranty or that the product I'm buying will last me a

69 Dalai Lama, *In My Own Words: An Introduction to My Teachings and Philosophy* (Hay House Inc., 2011), 2.
70 *The New Age of Aging: A Landmark Age Wave Study* (Age Wave, 2023).
71 *Quotable Women: A Celebration* (Running Press, 2004), p. 105.

lifetime. I wonder to myself, *Are they kidding? That warranty will likely outlive me.*

Our legacy is clear. We revolutionized music and organized festivals and concerts, like Woodstock, that were transformative. Hairstyles were cutting-edge, from men displaying shoulder-length locks to women wearing the boyish cut that put Vidal Sassoon on the map. In fashion, we rocked bell-bottoms and long, flowing dresses, often accessorized with a headband or granny glasses. A great number of us stood firm against the war in Vietnam and took strong measures to show our disapproval by burning draft cards and the American flag. Others fled the country to avoid being drafted to fight a war that made no sense to them. That was a sign of our times.

There are less recognized changes that occurred during our days in power. Seat belts in cars were made mandatory in the late sixties, saving countless lives. Personal computers and the World Wide Web were invented by boomers. We were environmentalists, hoping to save the Earth from further destruction caused by pollution, and we brought the notion of saving the planet into the mainstream. More attention was given to healthy eating habits, such as vegetarianism, and the popularity of homegrown vegetable gardens surged. Boomers were experimenting with microbiotic and macrobiotic food (not always healthy, as it turned out), while brown rice and tofu gained favor. Plant-based diets are more popular now than ever, and food awareness has grown dramatically because we took a position on causes, including what we kill to satisfy our culinary cravings.

And for many of us, we haven't forgotten how to impose ourselves into the conversations we deem important. We committed ourselves to moving mountains in the interest of humanity, even if it meant sustaining many casualties along the climb. We must continue to champion the causes that obviate human inequity, bring about political respect, and protect the health of our environment—along with all the countless other issues that are unjust and in need of healing.

And don't forget about you and your well-being along the way. So, continue to go forth with that same unrelenting hubris of our early boomer days. And do it in concert with a very large dose of chutzpah.

Antiquated

The taming winds
The roaring seas
The twinkling stars bring memories
Of the days when I was young and jolly
And when I sighed so melancholy
But the days grow fast
And the nights grow long
And I am in my old age where I belong
The years sped by like a streak of lightning
This part of maturing was actually frightening
But through the years I grew quite sage
And began to realize it was my old age

— Susan Dean, age 10

Acknowledgments

As any writer will tell you, writing is a singular journey. We are mostly steadied in front of a computer, tapping keys and hoping that our process will produce an epic piece of literature that will be lauded for its greatness. Well, at the very least, we hope that we will reach the finish line!

The process is multilayered: researching, documenting, reviewing, contemplating, and ruminating.

None of this is done without the help of others. Librarians have been invaluable in helping me source citations, articles, and books.

And to my early readers, I offer many thanks for your willingness to spend the time just because I asked. Your insights were meaningful and your opinions discerning.

To Sheina Goldman, my early research assistant who provided intelligent and useful information, I am so grateful that you showed up right on time.

And just when my exhaustive research had me down, Debbie Reinberg stepped in to offer her help, a selfless gesture without being asked. Thank you, Debbie, for lifting me back up.

And no writer should ever be so smug as to think she doesn't need an editor. I got lucky. Kristy Phillips came into my life to remind me that I was not alone, offering unwavering support. I embraced her with trust and eagerness. She did not disappoint. Thank you, Kristy, for being you—a new friend and literary sister.

And many thanks to the boomer generation for providing the color and context of these pages. It has been a spirited and riveting jaunt down memory lane.

In Loving Memory

1948–2025

For my friend Jeff Eagle, who brought so much joy
and laughter to my life.
You have been my sounding board and gentle
truth-teller through pages and years.
I am so grateful to have shared this journey with you.

About the Author

For me, life is about purpose, passion, and love.

We all have been blessed with special gifts. Some of us are fortunate to discover one or more of them early in life. From childhood, I've known that I have a gift for caring about, listening to, and helping others. I ultimately recognized that this was my purpose and my passion, and I have been sharing my gift all my life—personally and professionally.

Toward that end, my academic pursuits have included certifications in life coaching, grief and loss, and sexology, as well as a PhD in behavioral science. My unofficial writing career began in elementary school, and I have coalesced the totality of my background experience into writing this book.

Resources for Caring for Loved Ones

National Council on Aging

This national leader and trusted association helps people aged sixty and older. It works with nonprofit organizations, governments, and businesses to provide community programs and services. www.ncoa.org

AARP

A nonprofit, nonpartisan organization, AARP focuses on helping people fifty and older improve the quality of their lives. It offers information around topics such as healthy living, senior discounts, products, and news specific to seniors. www.aarp.org

Programs of All-Inclusive Care for the Elderly (PACE)

PACE helps people fifty-five and older by providing and coordinating all the types of care a senior living at home might need, such as medical care, personal care, rehabilitation, social interaction, medications, and transportation. www. pace4you.org

Eldercare Locator

As a free national service of the US Administration on Aging (AoA) and an initiative of National Association of Area Agencies on Aging, Eldercare Locator helps seniors find local resources, such as legal and financial support, caregiving services, home repair and modification, transportation, and more. www.eldercare.gov

Area Agencies on Aging (AAA)

This network of hundreds of organizations across America serves local seniors. Most focus on a specific geographic area of several neighboring counties, although a few offer services statewide. Each provides valuable information and assistance with programs that can help seniors. www.n4a. org

National Institute on Aging

The National Institute on Aging (NIA) is under the National Institute on Health and is dedicated to conducting research on aging as well as the health and well-being of older individuals. It's an important resource when it comes to health topics for the elderly and has helpful information and news regarding the nature of aging and the aging process, as well as diseases and conditions associated with growing older. www.nia.nih.gov

Meals on Wheels

Meals on Wheels operates in just about every community through more than five thousand independently run local programs. Each community runs its Meals on Wheels based on its needs and resources, but they are all dedicated and focused on providing seniors with nourishing and healthy meals in their own homes. www.mealsonwheelsamerica.org

MyHealthfinder

MyHealthfinder is a service under the U.S. Department of Health and Human Services. It provides links to helpful health-related websites, support, and self-help groups, in addition to government agencies and nonprofit organizations that assist seniors. www.healthfinder.gov

Guide to Long-Term Care for Veterans

For senior veterans living at home and enrolled in the VHA health care system, the Guide to Long-Term Service and Supports can provide helpful guidance to resources and information about long-term care. Their website explores the various forms of home, community-based, and residential care available to aging veterans. www.va.gov

The National Directory of Home Modification and Repair Resources

This useful resource can help you find qualified local services and professionals who can help you modify and renovate your home. www.homemods.org

www.ingramcontent.com/pod-product-compliance
Lightning Source LLC
Chambersburg PA
CBHW020245130626
46549CB00005B/2067